What driving instructors have to say about
Learn to Drive . . .

'This system is the most effective and professional package on the market . . .'

'It is mandatory reading for all my pupils. My successful pass rate is 94%.'

'All the requirements needed of a future driver are explained in this book.'

'Interesting, easy to follow pictures, a well illustrated book highlighting the significant key learning points.'

'I find the appointment/progress card invaluable, because it enables the pupil to have an accurate record of his or her progress, and also to know what their strengths and weaknesses are in each skill.'

Nigel Stacey: was also the author of 'Running Your Own Driving School' and 'The Driving Instructor's Handbook' (now approved and recommended by the Driving Standards Agency as reading material for driving instructors), both published by Kogan Page. Nigel's life's work lay in the training of hundreds of new drivers and driving instructors under his 'Autodriva' system. His influence in the driver training industry is still significant and he is a sad loss to those who recognised his professional expertise and valued him as a colleague and friend. Nigel's work and published materials benefited from contributions from his wife, *Margaret Stacey* who continues to operate under the 'Autodriva' name and to revise and update these publications since Nigel's untimely death. This work is based upon the Autodriva principles and is of benefit as a supplement to professional tuition.

First published in 1987
Reprinted 1987, 1988 (twice), 1989
Revised edition 1990
Reprinted 1991
Second edition published in 1993
Reprinted with revisions 1994
Reprinted 1995, 1996

Kogan Page Limited
120 Pentonville Road
London N1 9JN

British Library Cataloguing in Publication Data

A CIP record for this book is available from the British Library.

ISBN 0 7494 0716 6

Typeset by DP Photosetting, Aylesbury, Bucks
Printed and bound in Slovenia by Gorenjski tisk

LEARN TO
DRIVE
IN 10 EASY STAGES

MARGARET STACEY

Illustrated by Andy Rice

SECOND EDITION

KOGAN PAGE

About the Author

Margaret Stacey runs a successful driving instructor training establishment in Derbyshire. She is the co-author of the best-selling *Driving Instructor's Handbook* which is recommended to instructors by the Department of Transport; *Practical Teaching Skills for Driving Instructors*, now being used by new and experienced instructors for improving their teaching skills, and *The Advanced Driver's Handbook*, incorporated by many instructors throughout the UK and Ireland as part of their defensive driving courses. She has also co-authored *How to Pass the New Theory L Test* which covers the entire syllabus of the new theory test to be introduced in summer 1996. All of these titles are published by Kogan Page. Margaret also publishes a Home Study Programme for those studying for the Approved Driving Instructor examination and this is also used on licence by many other training establishments.

Acknowledgements

To my daughter, Sharon, for her continual love and support; and to Mark Harriman of Hunstanton for his contributions to this new version, based on his experience in using *Learn to Drive in 10 Easy Stages* with his pupils.

Contents

Introduction

This book has been written by Approved Driving Instructors recognised as leading tutors (driving instructor trainers).

It has been written to provide provisional licence holders with a comprehensive course in learning to drive and is linked to the Driving Standards Agency Recommended Syllabus for Learner Drivers.

You are recommended to take a course of lessons with a Department of Transport Approved Driving Instructor and supplement this with lots of practice.

One of the most common reasons for 'L' Test failure is insufficient practice and preparation. This book has been written to supplement your professional driving lessons and to provide guidance for those supervising your practice.

It shows you what to expect on your driving lessons; how to develop driving as a life skill; and what you need to know to pass your test.

Reducing the risk of becoming involved in accidents

A high percentage of newly-qualified drivers are involved in accidents. This book explains how to develop your control skills so that you will handle the car safely and efficiently. It teaches you to anticipate what other road users are likely to do so that you can reduce these risks.

Success rate of new drivers using this system

During field trials this training programme achieved driving test pass rates of over double the national average.

How to Use this Programme

Organising your course of training

Without a properly structured programme, learning to drive is often a haphazard, superficial and time-consuming process.

Learning the Highway Code by 'cramming' prior to taking the test can sometimes prove difficult, frustrating and a waste of time. By using this programme, you will learn how to apply the rules to different road situations.

Learn to Drive in 10 Easy Stages includes common-sense advice on everything from choosing your driving instructor to changing a wheel. The progressive stages will enable you to plan and pace yourself according to your own natural aptitude and ability.

Charting your progress

The systematic step-by-step programme is designed to take the panic and confusion out of practice and enable you to reduce the overall cost of lessons through more effective practice and use of your time.

Map your progress through the course by ticking the appropriate boxes.

The key points of the stage

Each stage identifies key learning points. Study the stage carefully before your driving lesson or practice. If practising privately it is extremely important that your supervisor studies each section with you.

Read the introduction to each stage

Follow the instructions in the introduction to the stage you are working on.

How to make learning the Highway Code rules easy

Learn the Highway Code rules listed in the introduction to each stage. In this way, you will be able to understand and apply them sensibly.

The Driving Standards Agency Syllabus for Learners

Driving Skills – Your Driving Test has been compiled by the Driving Standards Agency, whose motto is 'Safe Driving for Life'. It contains the syllabus recommended for learners. Read the pages listed in the introduction to each stage of *Learn to Drive* and make sure you get lots of practice at all of the skills involved.

Complete the checkpoint

Test your knowledge before practising in the car by completing the checkpoint. Tick the most appropriate answers in pencil and match them against those given at the foot of the page. You can record your scores in the appendix at the end of this book.

Using illustrations to help you understand

The illustrations in *Learn to Drive in 10 Easy Stages* will help you understand all of the skills, recognise risk sooner, predict potential danger and avoid conflict with less able drivers who were taught merely to pass the test.

Learning in stages

Keep to the stage sequence and make sure you have learned and practised all the points in each one before moving on to the next.

Using the guide as your personal record chart

When learning something new your instructor/supervisor should begin by giving you full instruction. As you improve, you should begin to carry out the various tasks with some assistance. Finally, you should be able to perform each skill without any help.

To chart your own progress, there are tick boxes at the end of each learning programme. You can also get your instructor and supervisor to help by filling in the 'comments' section.

I have read and understand this point

I can carry out this task with assistance

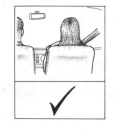

I can carry out this task reasonably well without help

Keep practising each skill until you and your instructor are happy with your performance and you are ready to proceed on to the next task.

In-car lessons and practice

Be sure to get enough lessons and practice on all of the points covered. If you are unsure of something, ask your instructor to go over the point again. Only move on to the next topic when you feel confident that you can carry out the skills reasonably well.

Maintaining concentration

When dealing with a new skill, limit the initial practising time to about 10 to 15 minutes. Then, take a three- or four-minute break to discuss your performance before you practise it again. This will help you maintain maximum concentration.

Recap at the start of each lesson

At the beginning of each practice period you should spend a few minutes revising what you did on your last lesson or practice session.

Keeping a check on appointments and progress

Your instructor may use a special appointment and progress record card. This will give you instant feedback of how you are progressing and show you the areas in which you need to revise and get more practice (see page 183–4).

You can also keep a record of your own progress by completing the 'Can do' statements table on page 181.

Before You Drive

Introduction

This section gives you advice on how to choose a driving school and about practice with friends and relatives. It also covers a few important things that you need to know before driving on the road.

To help you learn 'safe driving for life', you should supplement your driving lessons and practice by studying the following books: *The Highway Code*; *Driving Skills – Your Driving Test*; *Driving Manual* – the Department of Transport Manual; and *Know Your Traffic Signs*. All of these books are published by HMSO and you should be able to buy them from your driving instructor or any good bookshop.

As you progress through your course, study the sections in each of the above books that relate to what you are currently learning and practising.

Driving Skills – Your Driving Test gives you advice on learning to drive. It lists the subjects your instructor should be teaching you to ensure that: you will enjoy driving; learn the correct attitudes towards other road users; and will be able to handle your car safely and efficiently in all kinds of situations and conditions.

Read Section 1, pages 1, 2 and 3 and Section 4, pages 46–48.

Learn the Highway Code rules listed below before working through the main part of this section.

Rule 28	Vehicle condition and safety.
Rules 31–35	Health; eyesight; tinted optical equipment.
Rule 36	Supervision of learners.
Rule 38	Displaying 'L' plates.
Rule 39	Alcohol and the road user.
Rules 40–42	Seat belts.
Rules 131–132	Vehicle lights.
Rule 213	Animals in your car.

When you have studied the rules work through this stage. Complete the checkpoint by ticking the correct answers. Use a pencil so that you can rub out any incorrect ones.

Match your answers with those given at the foot of the page. Make a note of your scores in the appendix at the end of the book.

Rub out any wrong answers and revise that particular part of the stage. Try the questions again until you can get them all correct. Do not cheat!

Stage 1

Choosing a driving instructor

The only official qualification for giving driving tuition is Department of Transport Approved Driving Instructor. DoTADI is the correct abbreviation (ADI for short). Anyone using other initials or abbreviations for this qualification is out of date. Other initials denote membership of organisations that instructors will have paid to join, usually out of their own interest.

Your instructor's certificate

Your instructor should display a green certificate in the ▶ left-hand side of the car's windscreen. This is issued by the Driving Standards Agency and shows the official hexagonal badge bearing the instructor's photograph.

▼

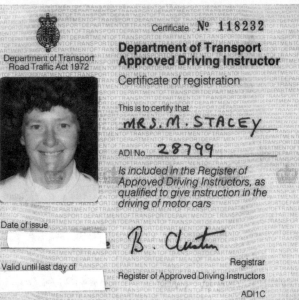

Some instructor's have a red triangular certificate on display bearing the words 'Licensed Trainee Driving Instructor'. This means that the instructor is not yet fully qualified and is learning the job while under the supervision of a qualified ADI. This may mean that, on occasion, the qualified instructor may sit in the back of the car to 'supervise' the trainee.

Ask around and go to an instructor who is known to achieve a high pass rate and who behaves professionally. Make an appointment to go and have a chat before committing yourself. This will establish whether or not you will feel at ease and be able to communicate with your instructor.

Ask for an outline of the course and check whether this covers the syllabus recommended by the Driving Standards Agency. If you are in doubt do not book any lessons or pay in advance.

'Safe driving for life'

Try to remember the importance of being taught to drive safely for the rest of your life. Your aim should be to cope, on your own, in today's busy traffic conditions on all types of road. The 'L' Test is only the basic minimum safety standard. Do not fall into the trap of making this your ultimate goal in the fewest possible number of lessons at the lowest cost.

Today's road and traffic conditions are such that learning to drive is very much more involved than it was 20 years ago. Don't be influenced by older drivers saying: 'I only needed six lessons before I passed.'

The number of lessons you need will depend not only on your driving instructor's skill and methods, but also on your age, your ability to learn, and how much regular practise you will be able to get.

Do I need to learn quickly?

Intensive courses can be very tiring, leading to loss of concentration and ineffective practice. If you need to learn fairly quickly, it is normally better to spread your lessons over four or five weeks rather than cram them into one- or two-week intensive courses. Before you consider such a course, you should bear in mind that no one can guarantee you a pass. Find out how many learners will be in the car together; how many hours practice you will get; and how much time will be spent in the classroom.

The cost of learning

Making the wrong choice of instructor may mean failed tests, more lessons and extra cost. Quality of tuition can vary as much as price. Go for quality and not quantity! For example: 24 lessons at £12 with a good instructor will cost you £288; 36 lessons at £10, with

someone not so good will cost you £360. As well as asking how much, ask how long each lesson will last and compare this with the price.

Are you already learning with an instructor?

If you are already learning to drive and are not quite sure about the quality of service you are getting, ask yourself the following questions:

Does my instructor:

- behave professionally?
- arrive on time for my lessons?
- check I am learning the Highway Code by asking questions?
- recap what I have learned on the previous lesson?
- tell me what we're going to do at the start of my lessons?
- explain new topics simply so that I can understand them?
- demonstrate difficult subjects?
- use illustrations to explain what is meant?

- give me praise and encouragement when I do things well?
- assess my performance and let me know how I am doing at the end of my lessons?
- give me guidance on what to read before my next lesson?
- provide me with an outline of the course?
- fill in my appointment/progress card on every lesson?
- give me a receipt?
- make me feel comfortable so that I can ask questions without feeling awkward?
- show an interest in what I am doing?
- help me to understand when I get things wrong?

If your instructor is doing the job properly you should be able to answer yes to most of these questions. If you can't, then you should try to discuss the problems. If you are offered no remedy, you should consider finding another instructor. (Remember it's your money and your choice!)

If you have a justifiable complaint, which your instructor refuses to remedy, write to: The Registrar of Approved Driving Instructors, Stanley House, Talbot Street, Nottingham NG1 5GU.

Practising with friends and relatives

The Driving Standards Agency recommend plenty of practice to supplement your driving lessons. However, it is best to have some lessons with a qualified driving instructor before practising with anyone else. Listen to your instructor's advice and only start practising when he or she says you are ready.

If you are practising with a friend or relative, by law your supervisor must be over 21 and have held a full UK driving licence for at least three years.

Not all drivers make good instructors and if you are taught bad habits at the start, they may stay with you for a long time. By studying this book your supervisor should be able to guide you along the path to success.

Close relatives are often too personally involved and tend to get over-anxious and agitated. If they tell you off unjustly, try to stay calm. Responding angrily only leads to further argument. ▼

When your instructor advises that you are ready for extra practice, fit an extra rear view mirror in your car for your supervisor to use. As your car won't have dual controls fitted, don't try to do too much too soon. Keep out of trouble by getting your supervisor to select routes that you can cope with. He/she should try to avoid problems by thinking well ahead.

Ask for instructions to be given clearly and in plenty of time so that you can carry them out comfortably. If things get out of hand your supervisor should be prepared to compensate, for example, with steering corrections or by applying the handbrake. Being a learner is no excuse for breaking the law – careless driving could result in a disqualification for both of you. Make sure you are able to stop quickly before you drive in traffic. If you really feel you can't cope ask your supervisor to take over.

Your instructor should tell you which parts of this book to study before going out to practise with your supervisor. Make sure you both understand what to do. If you're not quite sure, ask for a further explanation. If you find something really difficult, try something else for a while and go back to it later, or ask your instructor to work on it with you on your next lesson.

Avoid driving in really bad weather conditions during the early stages. There are too many other things for you to concentrate on. Although Sunday practice may be quite useful in the early and intermediate stages of learning, it usually fails to provide the kind of conditions you will experience during the test. When you are becoming more proficient, lessons and practice should be in busier conditions. Before you take your test, you should get some experience on as many different types of road as possible, and also practise driving in the dark.

Making it legal to drive

The minimum age for driving a small passenger or goods vehicle is normally 17. If you are in receipt of a mobility allowance the minimum age is 16. You can apply for the licence up to two months before you want it to commence. A provisional licence only allows you to drive motor cars and small vans under the supervision of an approved driving instructor or a qualified driver.

Remember it is illegal to give payment of any kind, either in money or goods, to anyone supervising your driving, unless they are on the Register of Approved Driving Instructors.

Make sure any vehicle you intend to drive is taxed. Check the expiry date on the tax disc in its window. Also

check that the vehicle is properly insured for you to drive it while you are learning. ▼

Alcohol and drugs

If you are talking medicines or drugs you should ask your doctor if they will affect your driving. Even some simple cough remedies can cause drowsiness. Read the directions carefully. If in doubt ask at the chemist.

▲

Alcohol is a drug that can make you feel over-confident and less aware of danger. It makes people think they can achieve the impossible and it blurs judgement of speed and distance.

Stage

1

Even small amounts of alcohol will slow down your reactions. It is a major cause of road accidents. If you drink the night before a lesson, the amount of alcohol in your body may still exceed the legal limit in the morning.

Is your vehicle roadworthy?

If the vehicle you are learning in is over three years old it must undergo an annual MOT test. Check the test certificate. Although this shows it passed the MOT on the day of the test, it doesn't mean that the vehicle is still in a roadworthy condition.

Before getting in, check the tyres to see whether they are flat or badly worn. Before driving away, check that the indicators, lights and horn are working.

Scratched or dirty windows make driving more difficult and tiring. Glare from bright sunlight, and the headlights of other cars, can become painful to the eyes. Use water and a soft cloth or leather to wash all windows inside and out. Also clean the mirrors and lights.

Condensation can restrict your vision, particularly in cold or damp weather. Use the demister and the rear screen heater to clear windows. A slightly open window will also help prevent condensation from re-forming. ▼

How to reduce distractions while learning

It is a good idea to visit the toilet before a lesson as any discomfort will affect your concentration. Get ready in plenty of time so that you can spend a few minutes relaxing before going out. This will help you collect your thoughts and prepare yourself mentally for the lesson. You should try to avoid arguments because they will put you in the wrong frame of mind for both driving and learning. ▼

Display 'L' plates so they can be seen clearly from the front and rear. The bumper is usually the best place to put them. You must not restrict your view of the road in front or behind. Do not put 'L' plates in the windows and remove any stickers or toy mascots that might restrict your view.

It is not normally a good idea to carry extra passengers during your first few lessons, because it can affect your concentration. If you must, organise them so they get in from the footpath side and sit them where they will not restrict your view in the mirror. ▼

Make sure that passengers do not obstruct your view

How to reduce distractions while driving

Children can get bored quickly and may make it difficult for you to concentrate on driving. If you must have them in the car when practising make sure they are restrained and kept under control. ▼

Before driving away, look around for loose articles that might distract you. Tidy up maps, papers or other articles lying about. If they move about when accelerating, slowing down or cornering they could distract you and cause an accident. ▼

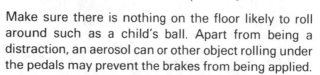

Make sure there is nothing on the floor likely to roll around such as a child's ball. Apart from being a distraction, an aerosol can or other object rolling under the pedals may prevent the brakes from being applied. ▼

The concentration needed when driving can be quite tiring. You will need plenty of fresh air to help you stay alert. During cold weather you should keep the in-car temperature comfortable, but not too warm.

Stage 1

Getting ready for your first lesson

Wear light, comfortable and loose fitting clothes. As most car heating systems are very effective, heavy coats are unnecessary and may restrict your arm movements when steering, making it difficult to turn the wheel. Avoid any tight fitting clothes, which may also restrict your body movements.

▼

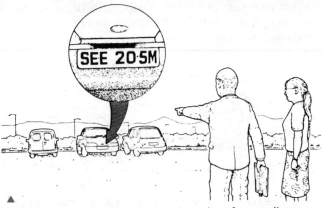

▲

Make sure you can read a number plate from a distance of at least 20.5 metres (67 feet). If you need glasses to do this you must also wear them for driving.

Flat shoes with enclosed or covered heels are usually best for driving. Heavy boots and fashion shoes are normally unsuitable and may make it awkward to control the pedals. ▼

Wear comfortable clothing

Fashion shoes are not suitable for driving

Checkpoint

Using a pencil, tick the box next to the answer you think is correct.

1. When choosing an instructor should you:

   (a) look for the one who is cheap?
   (b) ask round for recommendations?
   (c) look for the one with the newest car?

2. When you have applied for your provisional licence you:

   (a) must wait until you have received it.
   (b) must sign it in ink.
   (c) both (a) and (b).

3. The minimum age for driving a car is normally:

   (a) 16 years.
   (b) 17 years.
   (c) 18 years.

4. Before driving you should make sure:

   (a) the mirrors and windows are clean.
   (b) the lights and indicators work.
   (c) both (a) and (b).

5. Before driving you should make sure you can:

   (a) read a number plate at 67 feet.
   (b) read a number plate at 20.5 metres.
   (c) both (a) and (b).

6. Passengers should get in:

   (a) from the offside of the car.
   (b) from the nearside of the car.
   (c) passengers should not be present.

7. If you are taking prescribed medicines you should:

   (a) ask your doctor if it is safe to drive.
   (b) make up your own mind if you can drive.
   (c) ask your instructor if you can drive.

8. Cars used for lessons and practice should be:

   (a) taxed and properly insured.
   (b) in a roadworthy condition.
   (c) both (a) and (b).

9. 'L' plates must be displayed:

   (a) in the front and rear windows.
   (b) clearly to the front and rear.
   (c) on the front and rear bumper bars.

10. Your car should display:

    (a) a valid tax disc.
    (b) an MOT certificate.
    (c) an insurance certificate.

11. An MOT certificate is normally needed if:

    (a) your car is over one year old.
    (b) your car is over two years old.
    (c) your car is over three years old.

12. Small children should be:

    (a) kept under control.
    (b) secured in their seats.
    (c) both (a) and (b).

13. Loose papers should be:

    (a) kept in the glove compartment.
    (b) kept on the rear window shelf.
    (c) kept on the passenger seat.

14. Window stickers and toy mascots:

    (a) may restrict your view
    (b) may cause blind spots.
    (c) both (a) and (b)

15. If you have been drinking the night before your lesson:

    (a) you may still be over the legal limit for driving in the morning.
    (b) you may legally drive the following morning.
    (c) you will not be over the limit if you only had a few drinks.

16. Tinted windows improve vision:

    (a) when driving at night.
    (b) when driving in the daytime.
    (c) neither (a) nor (b).

17. Loose articles in the car could:

    (a) cause accidents.
    (b) distract the driver.
    (c) both (a) and (b).

Scores: 1st try [ ] 2nd try [ ] 3rd try [ ]
Record these scores in the appendix on page 179

Checkpoint answers

1. (b) **2.** (c) **3.** (b) **4.** (c) **5.** (c) **6.** (b)

7. (a) **8.** (c) **9.** (b) **10.** (a) **11.** (c) **12.** (c)

13. (a) **14.** (c) **15.** (a) **16.** (c) **17.** (c)

Stage **1**

Get to Know Your Car

Learn Highway Code Rule 140. Read pages 12–16 of *Your Driving Test*.

This lesson will give you a chance to get the feel of the controls and practise some simple exercises before moving away.

Make sure you understand and can carry out the following instructions before going on to Stage 3 and moving off:

The instruction	What it means
Cover the clutch	Place your left foot over the clutch pedal without touching it
Cover the brake	Place your right foot over the brake pedal without pressing it
Set the gas	Press the accelerator gently to increase the engine speed to a steady tickover ready for moving off
Find the holding point	Allow the clutch pedal to come up until you hear the engine slow down a little. Keep your foot still as soon as you hear the engine note change. This is often called the biting point
Handbrake ready	Put your hand on the handbrake ready to release it

After learning the Highway Code rule and the instructions listed above, work through this stage and complete the checkpoint before going out in the car.

As you work through this stage you will find other instructions that you should practise before moving away. For example: 'Move the gear lever into 1st' or 'Take the handbrake off'.

Complete the checkpoint by ticking the answer you think is correct. Use a pencil so that you can rub out any mistakes. Match your answers with those given at the foot of the page. Record your score in the special section in the appendix on page 179. Answer those questions that were incorrect again until you get them right. No cheating!

Stage 2

Getting into the 'cockpit drill' habit

1. Doors

Opening a door carelessly can put you or others in danger. It may force them to brake or swerve and could cause an accident.

Get in as quickly as you can, close the door and listen to make sure that any passengers have closed theirs. Check in the nearside and offside mirrors that the doors are flush with the bodyline of the car. You will be responsible for the safety of your passengers. A door not shut properly will rattle and may fly open as you ▶ drive along.

Also check the handbrake is firmly on.

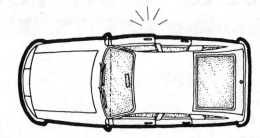

2. Seat

Adjust the seat and get comfortable. Sit up with your bottom well back in the seat and make sure you can see clearly ahead. If you need more height use a cushion. Make sure the head restraint is positioned correctly. Remember this is not a 'head rest'.

To position the seat correctly, push the pedal on the far left (the clutch) down to the floor. You should be able to do this without stretching. Don't get too close or you may find it awkward to let the pedal up and control the clutch.

Hold the wheel in the position shown in the diagram. ▶ Your arms should be slightly bent and your elbows clear of your body. Check to see if you can move your hands freely from the top of the wheel to the bottom. If you find this awkward, you could be sitting too close and may have to readjust the back rake of the seat.

3. Mirrors

Your instructor will teach you how to get into the mirror – signal – manoeuvre habit. Adjust the interior mirror so that you can see clearly to the rear with the minimum of head movement. Hold it as shown in the diagram keeping your fingers off the glass. Line up the ▶ top edge of the mirror along the top edge of the rear window; and the offside (driver's side) edge of the mirror down the right side of the window.

Adjust the door mirrors to reduce the blind areas to ▶ the sides of the car. You will need to use these before moving off, changing lanes or turning. Having adjusted the mirrors there will still be 'blind spots'. Your instructor should explain about these before you learn how to move off.

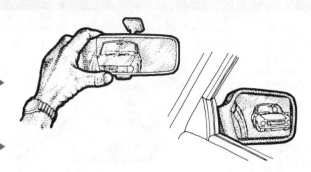

4. Seatbelts

Adjust and fasten your seatbelt. The law requires that all passengers wear seatbelts where fitted.

Children under 14 must wear seatbelts or be fastened securely in appropriate restraints. It is the driver's responsibility to ensure this.

Use child safety locks so that they can't open the doors from the inside. ▼

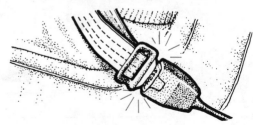

5. Handbrake and neutral

Before you switch on the engine, you must check that the car is secure. First of all check that the handbrake is on. This is sometimes referred to as the 'parking brake'. Ensure that it is raised to its highest position. This is to make sure that the car won't move when the engine is switched on. ▼

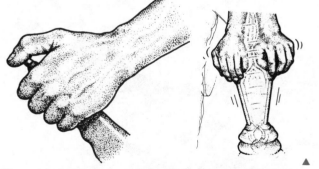

Now check that the gear lever is in the neutral position. Your instructor should show you how to make this check. When you move the lever from side to side, there should be plenty of movement. Checking that the car is not 'in gear' will ensure that it doesn't move when the engine is switched on.

Stage 2

How to start the engine

The starter or ignition switch is normally on or near the steering column and usually combines an anti-theft steering lock. ▼

▲

As you turn the key, look for the battery charging and oil pressure warning lights. Check these go out when the engine starts.

Turn the key gently to operate the starter, when the engine starts release the key. To stop the engine turn the key back to its original position.

▲

If the engine does not start, squeeze the accelerator (the pedal on the right) gently and try again. Do not pump the pedal as this can flood the engine and make starting even more difficult.

To start a cold engine, you may need to use the choke. This allows more fuel into the engine to make starting easier. However, this must be pushed in again as soon as the engine is warm. ▼

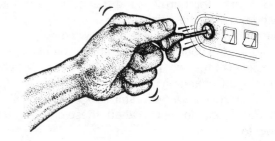

If your car runs on diesel, you may have to wait until the warning light goes out after turning on the electrical circuit before you can switch on the engine. ▼

Using the handbrake

The handbrake is used to secure the car when you park it or are stationary for more than a few moments. It is also used to help you time moving off into gaps in the traffic.

You must make sure the car has stopped before applying the handbrake. ▼

You must be able to apply and release the handbrake quickly, without looking down or wearing the ratchet mechanism (your instructor will explain this). Practise releasing and applying the handbrake while stationary.

First, press your footbrake (the middle pedal) firmly with your right foot. This will hold the car still while you practise. ▼

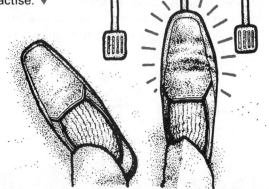

To release the handbrake put your hand on to it with your thumb on the button, pull the lever up slightly and press the button in. Keep the button pressed in while you lower the handbrake.

▼

▲

To put the handbrake on, press the button in and, keeping it in, pull the lever up firmly. Release the button to lock the brake on.

Stage 2

How to steer and operate the controls

Hold the wheel as in the diagram. Fold your palms loosely over the rim and rest your thumbs lightly up the flat of the wheel. Relax your shoulders and keep your arms free of your body. ▶

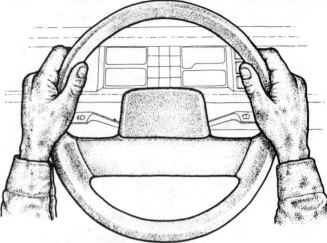

"...MUST LOOK AHEAD TO STEER....."

◀To steer accurately you must be able to operate the main controls without looking at them. Looking down will result in your car wandering from side to side.

Try to keep both hands on the wheel when braking or cornering.

Stage 2

Operating switches

The most frequently used switches, such as the direction indicators, lights and windscreen wipers, are usually on the column just behind the steering wheel.

Practise using them with your fingertips, keeping your hands on the wheel.

Other important switches include the horn, windscreen washer and demisters. You can learn about these when you have mastered the main controls towards the end of Stage 4.

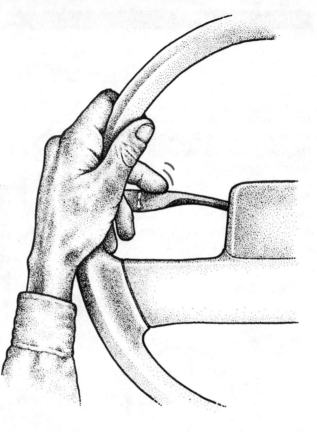

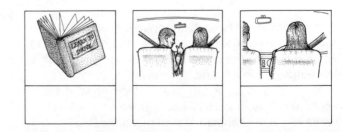

Stage 2

Using the gears

The lower gears give you lots of pulling power and quick acceleration.
1st gear is used for moving off, manoeuvring and for creeping slowly in traffic and at junctions.
2nd gear is used for moving off down some steep hills, building up speed after moving away and driving at low speeds. ▶

The higher gears allow you to drive comfortably at greater speeds. They are not so powerful and give less acceleration.
3rd gear is used to build up speed and when you need more power for climbing hills. It also increases your control when going down steep hills and dealing with some bends.
◀ 4th is the cruising gear.

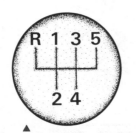

It is common to have four forward gears and one reverse. The neutral position allows the engine to run without turning the wheels. To check the gear lever is in neutral, move it from side to side.

Many cars have a 5th gear, which gives greater economy. This is normally only used on open roads when travelling constantly at higher speeds.

How to change gear

From neutral to 1st

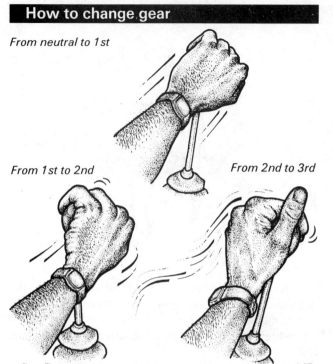

From 1st to 2nd

From 2nd to 3rd

When driving, you should be able to change gear without looking down at the lever. Practise this with the engine switched off and the clutch pressed down. Use a cupped palm to move the gear lever.

To practise finding 1st and 2nd, angle your palm and press the lever lightly away from you. Move it forwards to 1st gear then straight back to 2nd.

To select 3rd and 4th gears angle the palm towards you. Move the lever gently from 2nd into 3rd and finally 4th.

Now move the lever back to 3rd, to 2nd and then to 1st. Keep practising until you have perfected these movements.

Finally practise changing from 4th to 2nd and 3rd to 1st.

Driving an automatic car

Learning to start, steer and stop is much easier in automatic cars. The right foot should normally be used to control the accelerator and footbrake. There is no clutch to operate and after the initial gear selection has been made, all subsequent changes are carried out automatically. They are regulated by the car's speed and the pressure applied on the accelerator by the driver.

In some automatic cars, the driver may engage a fixed low gear for carrying out low speed manoeuvres.

When driving an automatic car, the handbrake has to be used more often to avoid its natural tendency to creep forwards.

Automatic transmission enables drivers to concentrate on the more important things, such as planning ahead and steering. It makes learning to drive easier, particularly for older or disabled people. The exercises set out in Stage 4 are made much simpler but practice should still be carried out using the accelerator and the brake with the right foot.

Your instructor should explain about the extra use of the handbrake and the different techniques used to control the car at low speeds.

If you pass your test in an automatic car, you will only be entitled to drive this type of vehicle.

Stage 2

Using the accelerator and footbrake

Position your right foot so that it will pivot comfortably between the accelerator and brake pedals. To do this, cover the brake pedal with your right foot. Without looking down or moving your heel, practise pivoting between these pedals. ▶

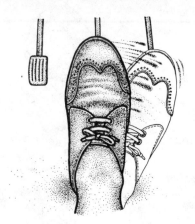

When you have found a comfortable position for your foot, get a feel for the brake pedal by pressing it lightly. The first pressure puts the brake lights on at the back of the car. When driving along, this will let anyone behind know you are braking. The harder you press the pedal, the more the car will slow down.

Now, start the engine. Remember your safety checks of: 'handbrake on and gear lever in neutral'.

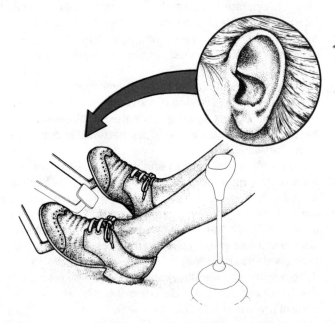

◀ Listen to the engine tickover speed and squeeze the accelerator gently until you hear a nice healthy purr. This is called setting the gas and you will need to do it when preparing to move off. Practise until you get it just right every time.

After moving off, you should notice that the car responds quite quickly to pressure on the accelerator when you are in the lower gears. Releasing the pressure will cause the car to slow down. This slowing effect is more pronounced in 1st and 2nd gears.

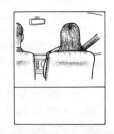

How the clutch works

The main purpose of the clutch is to connect and disconnect the power from the engine to the road wheels. It is needed so that changes can be made smoothly from one gear into another.

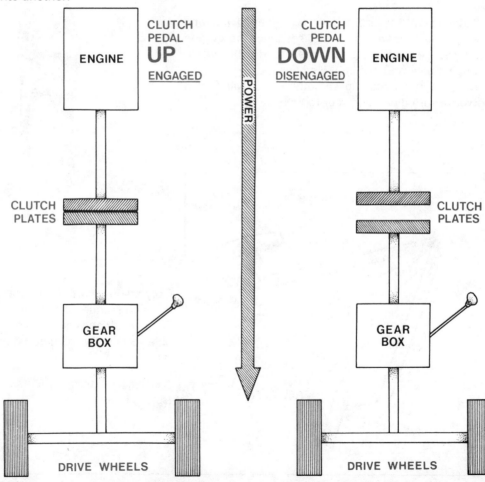

ENGINE

CLUTCH
PEDAL
UP
ENGAGED

CLUTCH
PEDAL
DOWN
DISENGAGED

ENGINE

POWER

CLUTCH
PLATES

CLUTCH
PLATES

GEAR
BOX

GEAR
BOX

DRIVE WHEELS

DRIVE WHEELS

Stage 2

To move off, change gear and stop, you should be able to use the clutch smoothly and without looking at your feet.

To begin with, cover the clutch with your left foot and then press it down. This will disconnect the engine from the gearbox. You will have to do this when changing gear and just before stopping.

Next let the pedal up smoothly. You will feel a powerful spring pushing your foot up.

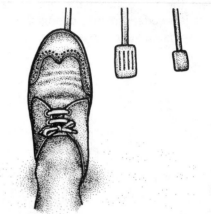

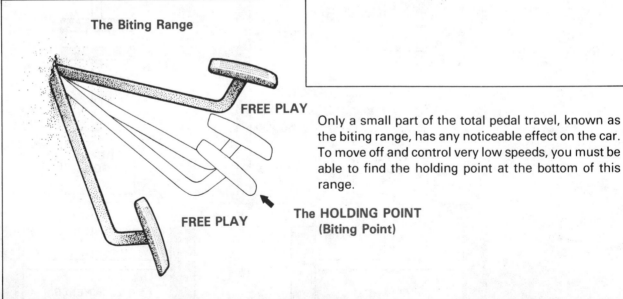

The Biting Range

FREE PLAY

FREE PLAY

The HOLDING POINT (Biting Point)

Only a small part of the total pedal travel, known as the biting range, has any noticeable effect on the car. To move off and control very low speeds, you must be able to find the holding point at the bottom of this range.

The holding point

The clutch consists of two friction plates that you must bring together smoothly when moving off. To do this you must first find the holding point. This allows the plates to touch lightly without driving the car. When the handbrake is released, and the clutch is at the holding point, the car should not move. This is known as a 'slipping clutch'. As the clutch is raised smoothly to the driving point it should creep at a very low speed.

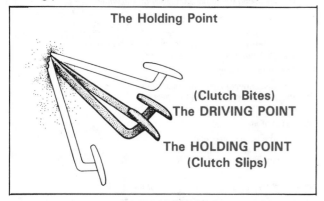

The Holding Point

(Clutch Bites)
The DRIVING POINT

The HOLDING POINT
(Clutch Slips)

How to find the holding (biting) point

To practise finding the holding point you must first start the engine. Remember to make sure the handbrake is on and the gear lever in neutral. Now push the clutch down. Select 1st gear and set the gas by squeezing the accelerator slightly until you hear a nice healthy purr; this is about half as fast again as the engine tickover speed.

Raise the clutch pedal slowly by bending your ankle. Keeping your heel down will give you more support and positive clutch control. It may feel a little awkward at first, particularly if you have small feet or are in a car with high pedals. Padding under the carpet may help to overcome these problems.

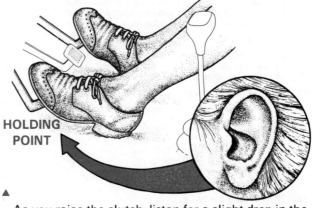

HOLDING POINT

As you raise the clutch, listen for a slight drop in the engine speed. When you hear or feel this, you have found the holding point and should keep the pedal still.

After keeping your foot still for a couple of seconds or so, push the clutch pedal down again and release the accelerator. Put the gear lever into neutral and relax your feet.

Practise this exercise until you can find the holding point fairly quickly every time.

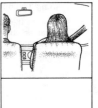

Stage 2

Checkpoint

Using a pencil, tick the box next to the answer you think is correct.

1. The correct 'cockpit drill' sequence is:

   (a) doors/seat/mirrors/seatbelt/handbrake/neutral.
   (b) doors/mirrors/seat/handbrake/neutral/seatbelt.
   (c) handbrake/neutral/doors/seat/seatbelt/mirrors.

2. Seatbelts should be:

   (a) only worn if you think it is necessary.
   (b) worn by passengers in the front and rear.
   (c) worn only children under 14 years of age.

3. The most frequently used switches are:

   (a) positioned near the steering wheel.
   (b) positioned on the dashboard.
   (c) positioned near the handbrake.

4. The right foot is used to control:

   (a) the clutch and brake pedals.
   (b) the clutch and accelerator pedals.
   (c) the accelerator and brake pedals.

5. The left foot operates:

   (a) the brake and clutch pedals.
   (b) the clutch pedal only.
   (c) the accelerator only.

6. To steer you must concentrate on:

   (a) what your hands are doing.
   (b) where you want the car to go.
   (c) objects you want to avoid.

7. Before starting the engine you should:

   (a) pull out the choke.
   (b) check the fuel level.
   (c) check the handbrake and neutral.

8. Starting the engine while in gear may:

   (a) cause the car to move.
   (b) damage the handbrake.
   (c) damage the accelerator.

9. The clutch:

   (a) transmits power to the gearbox.
   (b) controls the speed of the engine.
   (c) controls the speed of the car.

10. Door mirrors:

    (a) reduce blind spots to the rear and sides.
    (b) completely compensate for all blind spots.
    (c) need only be used by experienced drivers.

11. The choke is used:

    (a) to help start the engine when hot.
    (b) to help start the engine when cold.
    (c) only on automatic and diesel cars.

12. Two hands should be on the steering wheel:

    (a) always.
    (b) only when driving in a straight line.
    (c) when braking and cornering.

13. Direction indicators should be operated:

    (a) without releasing the steering wheel.
    (b) with either hand.
    (c) by taking the hand completely off the wheel.

14. The handbrake should be applied:

    (a) every time you stop the car.
    (b) when you are stopped for more than a moment.
    (c) only when you are leaving the car parked.

15. In neutral, the engine is:

    (a) disconnected from the road wheels.
    (b) connected to the road wheels.
    (c) ticking over at a very high rate.

16. 1st gear is:

    (a) the least powerful gear.
    (b) the most economical gear.
    (c) the most powerful gear.

Scores: 1st try [ ]   2nd try [ ]   3rd try [ ]

Record your scores in the appendix on page 179

Checkpoint answers

1. (a)   **2.** (b)   **3.** (a)   **4.** (c)   **5.** (b)   **6.** (b)

7. (c)   **8.** (a)   **9.** (a)   **10.** (a)   **11.** (b)   **12.** (c)

13. (a)   **14.** (b)   **15.** (a)   **16.** (c)

Instructor's/supervisor's comments: ....
....
....

Starting to Drive

Introduction

Make sure you have learned and practised the exercises in Stage 2 and can carry out the skills reasonably well. In Stage 3 you will be learning how to move off, change gear, steer and stop.

It is better to practise the points covered in this lesson with your driving instructor before practising privately. A professional instructor will drive you to a quiet area so that you can learn the basic car control skills before going into traffic. Housing estates or roads with lots of parked cars and junctions are unsuitable for initial practice.

An instructor will talk you, step by step, through each skill until you can manage on your own. Listen carefully for any directions and concentrate on what your instructor is telling you to do. Try to avoid talking while you are moving unless you need to ask a specific question in relation to what you are doing.

A professional instructor will give you plenty of warning for turns, but when practising with friends or relatives you may find yourself short of time. If this happens, tell your supervisor to give you a little more time. Although it is normally considered to be polite to look at people when they are talking to you, don't do it when you are driving. Try to keep your eyes on the road ahead. Directions should be given clearly as follows:

1. I want you to take the next road on the left.
2. Take the second road on the right, this is the first.
3. At the end of the road turn left.
4. Would you turn right at the end of the road, please?

Before going out to practise the skills in this Stage, learn the Highway Code rules listed below:

Rules 48–49	Moving off and the normal driving position.
Rules 137–139	Parking.

Read pages 17 and 37 of *Your Driving Test*

Work through this section of the book and complete the checkpoint before your driving lesson. Match your answers with those given and rub out any you get wrong. Revise any part of the section you feel you don't understand.

Remember to record your score in the special section at the back of the book.

The mirror-signal-manoeuvre routine

It's never too soon for you to start getting into the mirror–signal–manoeuvre routine.

Using the mirror

You should check your mirror well before signalling and making any changes in your speed or direction. Check it before: moving off, accelerating, pulling out to pass parked cars, overtaking, positioning to turn, and slowing down or stopping.

Using your mirrors properly will enable you to act on what you see in them. Your instructor should teach you how to do this.

Giving signals

You should give a signal if it will help to warn or inform any other road user of your intentions. The signals you will mainly be using at this stage are the brake lights and direction indicators.

The red brake lights at the rear of your car will come on automatically when you press the footbrake. They tell drivers behind that you are slowing down. If you see brake lights on a vehicle ahead you should check your mirror and start easing off the accelerator in preparation for braking.

Indicator lights flash at the front and rear of your car to let others know that you intend to change direction or stop. Signals should be given in plenty of time so that others may respond to them.

Making a manoeuvre

'Manoeuvre' is the word used to describe any change that you make in your position or speed. It also involves continually looking and assessing what's happening

around you so that your actions don't affect anyone else.

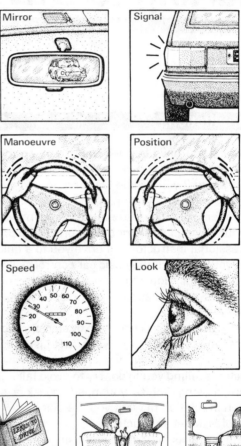

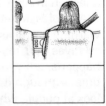

How to move off

You should normally use 1st gear for moving off except when pulling away down a steep hill.

Get ready to move: take an initial look to the front and in the mirrors for traffic and pedestrians and then get ready to move.

To prepare to move, push the clutch down and select 1st gear. Find the holding point and keep the clutch still. ▶

Check it's safe to move: by looking in the interior and door mirrors. To be 100 per cent sure, look round for other road users in your blind spots. Be prepared to wait. Decide if you need to signal. This should be given if it will help to warn or inform others that you intend moving away. ▶

To move away: have the handbrake ready to release. You must be sure it's safe before letting your car move. You can time the moment for moving with the release of the handbrake. This should allow the car to creep forwards. If the car doesn't move, let the clutch up a little more. ▶

To increase speed, press the accelerator gently and when the car is moving, start easing the clutch up slowly. Continue to press the accelerator gently as you raise the clutch smoothly to the top.

You will need to change into 2nd gear soon after moving off.

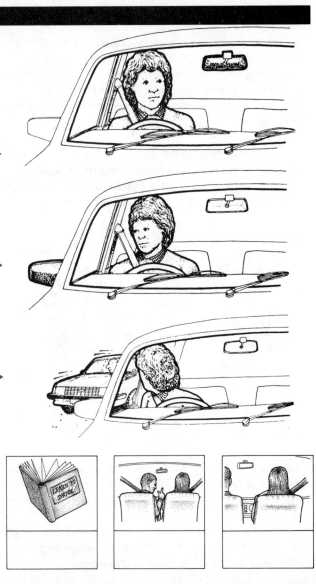

Stage 3

To change gear

1st gear provided the power you needed for pulling the weight of the car away. You don't need so much power now so you need to change into 2nd. This will allow you to accelerate from the low speed. Remember, when selecting 1st and 2nd gears, to angle your palm away from you.

Preparing to change (from 1st to 2nd): grip the wheel a little more firmly with your right hand and, keeping your eyes on the road, cup your hand over the gear lever ready. Cover the clutch without touching it.

From 1st to 2nd   *From 2nd to 3rd*

After accelerating in 2nd to about 20 mph, change to 3rd. Use this gear to build up speed to about 30 mph, then change into 4th. For 3rd and 4th gears, remember to angle your palm towards you.

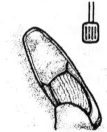

It is inadvisable to drive for prolonged periods with the clutch covered. As soon as you get into 4th gear place your left foot on the floor away from the pedal.

To change gear (from 1st to 2nd): push the clutch down quickly and take your foot off the gas pedal at the same time. Using gentle pressure, move the gear lever from 1st into 2nd.

Raise the clutch smoothly to the top and then press the accelerator gently to increase the engine speed.

Put your left hand back on to the wheel.

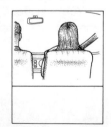

How to steer and judge your driving position

You are likely to drift towards things you look at. Look well ahead to where you want the car to go.

Don't look at the kerb or the road just in front of the bonnet. Avoid staring at nearby objects, it will only make you steer towards them. Try to drive about a metre (2 to 3 feet) out from the kerb and look in the direction you want the car to go. Plan your course well ahead by memorising the position of any obstructions. Rely on your side vision to sense your position in the road and to judge the clearance you are leaving between your car and parked vehicles. ▼

▶

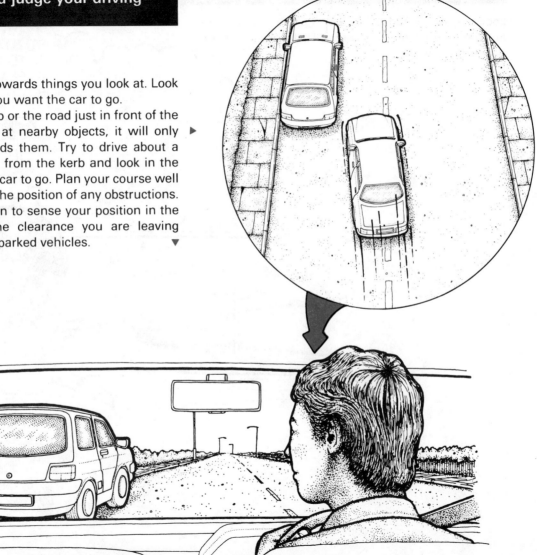

How to steer and drive at a safe speed

Look into the distance for road signs or obstructions
and be prepared to slow down well before reaching any
bends or junctions. ▼

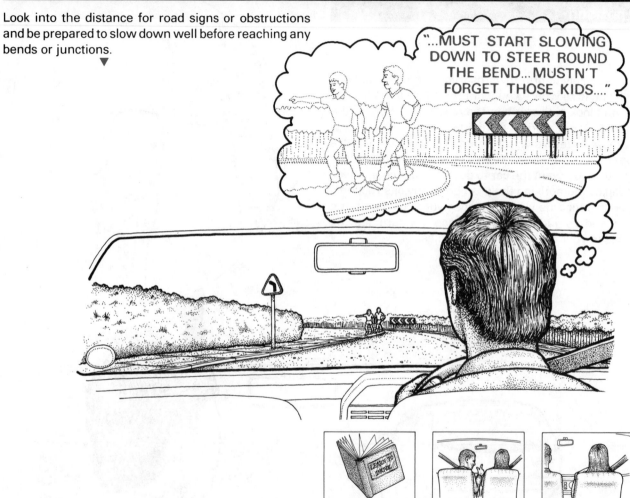

"...MUST START SLOWING DOWN TO STEER ROUND THE BEND... MUSTN'T FORGET THOSE KIDS...."

Stopping and parking

Try to park well away from bends, junctions and hilltops. These are all places where the driver's view is already restricted.

Parking your car in an unsafe place will increase the danger by forcing others on to the wrong side of the road when they can't see approaching traffic. ▶

Find a straight part of the road and, putting the mirror–signal–manoeuvre routine into practice, stop as close to the kerb as you can without touching it.

First of all, check for following traffic and, if necessary, signal to tell them what you are going to do (ie give a left signal).

The secret of stopping smoothly is to brake early. Brake gently at first, gradually building up into a firm pressure until you feel the car slowing down slightly more than you think is necessary. Gradually ease some pressure from the brake to let the car roll gently to a stop. Keep both hands on the wheel while you are braking.

Remember to push the clutch down just before you stop and keep it down until you have applied the handbrake and put the gear lever into neutral. Rest your feet and switch off the engine.

*Do not park
dangerously*

Before you open the door to get out of the car, look round for other road users who may be hidden in the blind spot.

▼

Stage 3

How to stop within the distance you can see is clear

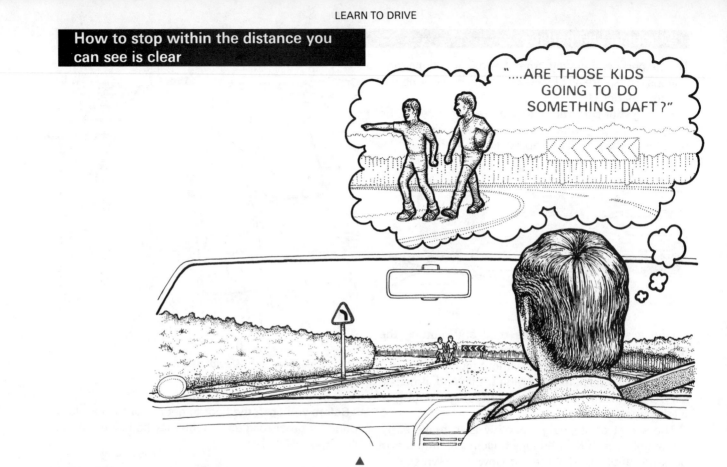

"....ARE THOSE KIDS GOING TO DO SOMETHING DAFT?"

Look, and be ready to slow down, for other road users who might move into the road or turn across your path. Watch out for people and vehicles moving from behind obstructions.

Checkpoint

Using a pencil, tick the box next to the answer you think is correct.

1. The term: 'Set the gas' refers to:

    (a) the accelerator and engine speed. ☑
    (b) the clutch and its biting range. ☐
    (c) the ignition switch. ☐

2. To prepare for moving off you should:

    (a) select 1st gear and then push the clutch down. ☐
    (b) push the clutch down and then select 1st gear. ☑
    (c) set the engine speed and then push the clutch down. ☐

3. To find the holding point you should:

    (a) listen to the engine speed. ☑
    (b) look down at your feet. ☐
    (c) keep your hand on the gear lever. ☐

4. To control the clutch smoothly, it helps if you:

    (a) keep your heel down. ☐
    (b) find the holding point. ☐
    (c) both (a) and (b). ☑

5. Before moving you should:

    (a) check the interior mirror. ☐
    (b) check the offside door mirror. ☐
    (c) both (a) and (b). ☑

6. Before moving off you should also:

    (a) check your door is closed. ☐
    (b) look round over your shoulder. ☑
    (c) check the handbrake is on. ☐

7. When preparing to change gear you should:

    (a) position your hand on the gear lever. ☐
    (b) cover the clutch pedal. ☑
    (c) both (a) and (b). ☐

8. To move the gear lever smoothly you should:

    (a) cup your hand to face towards the gear position. ☑
    (b) grip the gear lever as tightly as you can. ☐
    (c) push the lever as quickly as you can. ☐

9. To steer accurately you should look:

    (a) well ahead at where you want the car to go. ☑
    (b) towards the kerb to give you a reference point. ☐
    (c) towards the white line in the centre of the road. ☐

10. In normal driving you should steer:

    (a) about 3 feet or 1 metre away from the kerb. ☑
    (b) as close to the kerb as you can without hitting it. ☐
    (c) about one foot from the white line. ☐

11. Parking near bends and hill crests:

    (a) puts other road users at risk. ☐
    (b) may cause a head-on collision. ☐
    (c) both (a) and (b). ☑

12. The correct driving sequence is:

    (a) signal–manoeuvre–mirror. ☐
    (b) mirror–signal–manoeuvre. ☑
    (c) signal–mirror–manoeuvre. ☐

13. Brake lights come on automatically when:

    (a) the direction indicators are used. ☐
    (b) the footbrake is pressed. ☑
    (c) the accelerator is released. ☐

14. To stop smoothly and accurately you should:

    (a) brake smoothly and early. ☐
    (b) keep both hands on the wheel. ☐
    (c) both (a) and (b). ☑

15. Before leaving your car should you:

    (a) switch the engine off. ☐
    (b) apply the handbrake. ☐
    (c) both (a) and (b). ☑

16. The correct pressure sequence for smooth braking is:

    (a) hard–light–hard. ☐
    (b) light–firm–light. ☑
    (c) light–firm–hard. ☐

17. If you park near junctions you will:

    (a) make it difficult for other drivers to look. ☐
    (b) make it difficult for pedestrians to cross. ☐
    (c) both (a) and (b). ☑

18. Before leaving your vehicle parked you should:

    (a) ensure the handbrake is on. ☐
    (b) switch off the engine and headlights. ☐
    (c) both (a) and (b). ☑

Scores: 1st try ☑ 2nd try ☐ 3rd try ☐

Remember to record your scores in the appendix on page 179

Checkpoint answers

1. (a)	**2.** (b)	**3.** (a)	**4.** (c)	**5.** (c)	**6.** (b)
7. (c)	**8.** (a)	**9.** (a)	**10.** (a)	**11.** (c)	**12.** (b)
13. (b)	**14.** (c)	**15.** (c)	**16.** (b)	**17.** (c)	**18.** (c)

Stage 3

Instructor's/supervisor's comments: ....
....
....

Methodical Driving Practice

Introduction

Up to now, your instructor has been telling you what to do and when to do it. This should have helped you to get things right first time and build up your confidence in handling the car.

Stage 4 consists of a series of exercises designed to help you to start doing more for yourself. Practise the steps in each exercise separately until you can carry them out without help. It is important that you spend sufficient time developing your car control skills before attempting to drive where there is other traffic. This way, what you need to do inside the car will become more automatic, so that you can spend more time concentrating on what is happening on the road.

When you can carry out the exercises in this section you can also start practising the manoeuvres described in Stage 6.

A professional instructor will always keep a look out for other road users. This allows you to practise the exercises in safety until you are able to make all the observations for yourself. ▼

If you are learning with friends or relatives, they must help you by observing the road and traffic situation to ensure safety throughout. The extra mirror should help with this.

Before going out to practise learn the following HIghway Code rules:

Rules 44–47	Signs and signals.
Rules 50–53	Driving along.
Rule 57	Stopping distances.
Rules 109–110	Junction controls.

Read pages 17, 18 and 24 of *Your Driving Test*.

Work through this section of the book and complete the checkpoint before your lesson or practice session. If you get any wrong, revise the weak points.

Stage 4

Exercise 1 – How to control the car at low speeds and move off smoothly

Practise each step of this exercise on a fairly wide road. Find a safe position on a slight uphill slope and stop about a foot away from the kerb. Practise each step until you can carry it out smoothly with the car under control.

Step 1 – Finding the holding point

With the engine running, select 1st gear, set the gas and find the holding point. If there are no other road users nearby, release the handbrake. Keep your feet still and hold the car stationary for two or three seconds.

If the car moves forwards, press the clutch down a little. If it rolls back, keep calm and raise the clutch slightly. ▶

Step 2 – Moving off slowly with a slipping clutch

Follow the procedure in Step 1 and then raise the clutch slightly until the car moves forwards.

Now press the clutch down slightly and try to creep forwards very slowly without stopping.

▼

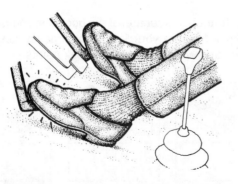

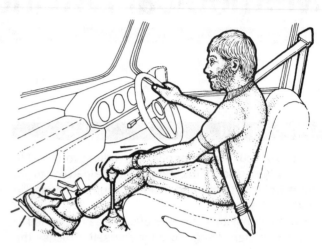

Step 3 – How to regain control when rolling backwards

Over-anxiety about rolling back can be a major cause of loss of control on uphill junctions. This exercise should help to increase your confidence by showing how easy it is to regain control and stop the car rolling.

Follow the procedure in Step 1 and then push the clutch down slightly until the car starts rolling backwards. Let it roll for two or three yards. To regain control, raise the clutch gradually until you can feel the car stopping.

It is important to control the clutch very gently. If you let the pedal up too far or too quickly it may stall the engine or cause the car to jump forwards. At junctions this could be more dangerous than rolling back a little.

Step 4 – How to move off quickly

Follow the procedure in Steps 1 and 2 until the car is creeping forwards.

To accelerate and move away quickly you should start gently pressing the accelerator and then slowly raise the clutch. Continue accelerating gently as you let the clutch up.

If the car jerks, you need to let the clutch up more slowly or press the accelerator a little more. If the engine roars, use less pressure on the accelerator or let the clutch up a little further.

Remember to change into 2nd gear as soon as possible after moving off.

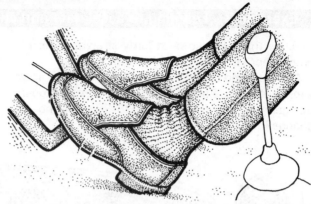

Gently press down the accelerator and slowly raise the clutch

Exercise 2 – How to control low speeds when moving away downhill

When moving off downhill there are times, such as in heavy traffic, at junctions, or when moving out from behind parked vehicles, when you will need to restrain the speed and move off very slowly. To do this you must keep the clutch just below the holding point and use the footbrake to prevent the car rolling away too quickly.

To practice, park on a quiet road facing downhill. Select 1st gear, or 2nd if on a steep slope. Apply the footbrake to hold the car and release the handbrake.

If there are no road users nearby, raise the clutch to just below the holding point. You will have to 'feel' for this as the change in the engine note will be less noticeable. Gradually ease the footbrake off to let the car roll slowly forwards. Raise the clutch smoothly all the way to the top and gently accelerate away.

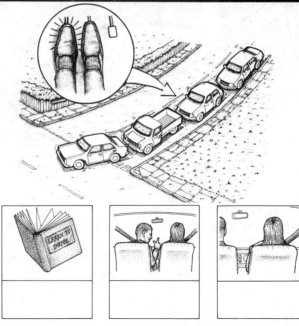

Exercise 3 – Learning to accelerate and change up through the gears

Practise this exercise on a fairly straight, wide road where there is little or no other traffic.

Move off and change into 2nd gear as soon as you can. Accelerate to about 15–20 mph, then change into 3rd gear. Accelerate in 3rd to 25–30 mph and then change into 4th.

▲

After completing the exercise, find a safe position and park at the side of the road. Discuss your performance with your supervisor to find out where you can improve. Practise until you feel confident about changing up through the gears on your own.

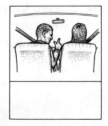

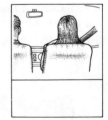

Exercise 4 – Learning to brake and change down through the gears

To practise this exercise you will need to move off and build your speed up until you are driving at about 30 mph in 4th gear. Your supervisor should help by keeping a look out, making sure it is safe for you to carry out each step of the exercise.

Step 1 – Changing down through the gears

Check the mirror to make sure it is safe. Brake gently to slow the car down to about 20 mph. Release the brake and change into 3rd gear. Check the mirror again and, if safe, reapply the brake gently and slow down to about 10 mph. Release the brake and change into 2nd gear.

Check the mirror and, if safe, build up your speed, changing up through the gears, until you are travelling at about 30 mph again. Keep practising the exercise until you feel confident.

Step 2 – Changing from 4th into 2nd gear

Move off and build up your speed until you are travelling at about 30 mph in 4th gear. Check the mirror to make sure it is safe and brake gently to slow the car down to about 10 mph. Release the brake and change from 4th gear into 2nd.

If safe, build up your speed, changing up through the gears, until you reach about 30 mph again. Keep practising until you can carry out the exercise smoothly and confidently.

Step 3 – Changing from 3rd to 1st gear

To practise this exercise you will need to move off and build up your speed until you are driving along at about 20 mph in 3rd gear.

If safe behind, brake gently to slow the car down until you have almost stopped. Push the clutch down, keep it down and release the brake so the car keeps rolling forwards very slowly. Just before the car stops, change from 3rd gear into 1st.

When safe, move off again and accelerate, changing up through the gears until you reach about 20 mph in 3rd so that you can practise again. Keep practising the exercise until you feel confident.

▼

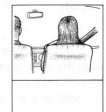

Stage

4

Exercise 5 – How to stop smoothly at a given point

To practise this exercise you must find a fairly straight quiet road with plenty of distinctive features such as telegraph poles, or trees. The object will be to stop with your front bumper level with one of these. You will need lots of practice so that you can consistently bring ▶ the car to a smooth stop at the required place.

When safe, move off and build up your speed to about 25–30 mph with 3rd or 4th gear selected. Your supervisor should look ahead and select your stopping place. Check your mirror and, when safe, cover the

brake. This will have a slight braking effect as the engine begins to slow down. Use this to help you judge ◀ how much braking pressure you will need. To begin with, squeeze the brake very gently. Gradually press it harder until you appear to be stopping short of the required position.

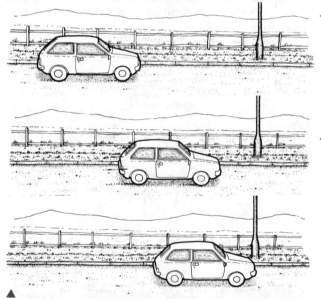

◀ Gradually ease the braking pressure and push the clutch down. This will allow the car to roll up to the stopping point. Select 1st gear ready for moving away.

▲
As the car comes to a rest with the front almost level with the stopping point, set the gas and find the holding point. Take care not to let the clutch up too far. Hold the car still for a second or two while checking it is safe to move away.

Exercise 6 – How to stop in an emergency

Anticipation helps you to avoid emergencies. You will learn more about this in Stage 8.

For now all you need to know is that the earlier you ▶ spot any possible danger, the sooner you can act on it. Taking early precautions, such as slowing down, will reduce the likelihood of needing to brake hard at the last moment.

Even experienced drivers sometimes find themselves having to stop quickly because they have failed to anticipate danger, or something completely unexpected happens.

Make sure *you* can stop quickly before you go into heavy traffic.

Practise the emergency stop on a quiet, fairly wide and straight road.

Before you move away your supervisor *must* demonstrate the signal to be given for the stop and, after moving away, ensure there are no other road users about before giving it.

In a real emergency there is little time to use the mirrors before braking. Make sure you are using them often as you drive along so that you are aware of what is happening behind.

Step 1 – Braking firmly to a stop

Your first attempts at stopping quickly should be carried out at fairly low speeds. Just practise stopping with a little more than the pressure needed for a normal stop.

When the signal to stop is given, respond at once and pivot quickly to the brake. Press the brake firmly but progressively and keep a firm hold of the wheel with both hands. Wait until the car has nearly stopped

before pushing the clutch down. Pushing it down too soon can increase the stopping distance and the risk of skidding. After coming to a complete stop, put the handbrake on.

Remember you were in your normal driving position on the road before you stopped. Check that it is safe all around the car before you move away again.

Stage 4

Step 2 – Stopping quickly as in an emergency

Repeat the previous exercise, gradually increasing the speed and the braking pressure until you can stop the car quickly, and without skidding or swerving. It may feel as if your car travelled a long way before coming to a stop. Read about stopping distances in your Highway Code and remember that in wet conditions these will be much longer. Use a lighter pressure on the brake or you may lock the wheels and skid.

Exercise 7 – Steering practice and checking the instruments

Step 1 – Anticipating when to turn the wheel

Find a quiet road with some sharp bends.

When approaching left bends, move your left hand towards the top of the wheel ready to pull it down to steer round the curve in the road.

When approaching right bends, move your right hand towards the top of the wheel ready to pull it down to steer round the curve in the road.

Step 2 – Steering with one hand

Although you should keep both hands on the wheel as much as possible, there are times when you need to change gear or operate the lights, wipers and other controls.

Find a straight, quiet road where you can steer with one hand while you practise using these controls. You can also practise winding the windows up and down.

Step 3 – Giving arm signals

Practise giving arm signals for left and right turns and for slowing down.

Step 4 – When to check the instruments

The instruments help to keep you informed of the condition of your car. Ignoring warning lights can result in breakdowns or serious damage.

When checking them, look well ahead and glance quickly at one instrument at a time. Only do this when there is nothing much happening on the road and you can spare the time.

You should stop and get help if the brake warning light comes on; if the temperature gauge shows the engine is overheating; or if the oil pressure is low.

Find out from your car's handbook what all of the symbols on the dashboard mean.

▼

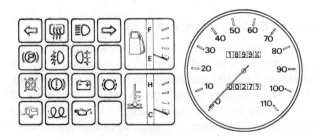

Checkpoint

Using a pencil, tick the box next to the answer you think is correct.

1. When travelling at 30 mph your thinking distance is:

    (a) 30 feet/9 metres. ☐
    (b) 45 feet/14 metres. ☐
    (c) 75 feet/23 metres. ☐

2. When travelling at 30 mph your braking distance is:

    (a) 30 feet/9 metres. ☐
    (b) 45 feet/14 metres. ☐
    (c) 75 feet/23 metres. ☐

3. When travelling at 30 mph your overall stopping distance is:

    (a) 30 feet/9 metres. ☐
    (b) 45 feet/14 metres. ☐
    (c) 75 feet/23 metres. ☐

4. When travelling at 40 mph your overall stopping distance is:

    (a) 75 feet/23 metres. ☐
    (b) 120 feet/36 metres. ☐
    (c) 240 feet/73 metres. ☐

5. When travelling at 70 mph your overall stopping distance is:

    (a) 175 feet/53 metres. ☐
    (b) 245 feet/75 metres. ☐
    (c) 315 feet/96 metres. ☐

6. Signs giving orders are mostly:

    (a) rectangular. ☐
    (b) triangular. ☐
    (c) circular. ☐

7. On wet roads the gap between you and the car ahead should:

    (a) be at least doubled. ☐
    (b) remain the same. ☐
    (c) be at least quadrupled. ☐

8. You should only park:

    (a) where it is convenient for you. ☐
    (b) where it is legal. ☐
    (c) in car parks. ☐

9. When moving off down hill you should:

    (a) always use 1st gear. ☐
    (b) use 1st or 2nd gear. ☐
    (c) never use 1st gear. ☐

10. The brake lights on your car should mean:

    (a) I am going to stop. ☐
    (b) I am slowing down or stopping. ☐
    (c) I intend to turn. ☐

11. A solid white line across the end of the road means:

    (a) you must stop at the stop sign. ☐
    (b) give way at the traffic signal. ☐
    (c) you may go if the way is clear. ☐

12. Double broken lines across the end of the road mean:

    (a) stop at the stop sign. ☐
    (b) give way to traffic in the major road. ☐
    (c) stop at the give way line. ☐

13. Double solid lines along the centre of the road means:

    (a) do not overtake. ☐
    (b) do not cross the lines. ☐
    (c) cross the line only when you can see it is clear. ☐

14. Long white lines with short spaces in the centre of the road:

    (a) provide drivers with warning of a hazard. ☐
    (b) mean that you must not cross this line. ☐
    (c) mean you may overtake if it is safe. ☐

15. To stop in the shortest distance you should:

    (a) brake as hard as you can and push the clutch down at the same time. ☐
    (b) brake until the wheels lock up. ☐
    (c) brake firmly and press the clutch down just before you stop. ☐

16. While braking in an emergency situation you should:

    (a) keep both hands on the wheel. ☐
    (b) brake hard and change down to a lower gear. ☐
    (c) brake hard and do not push the clutch down. ☐

17. Not keeping a regular check on the car's instruments may result in:

    (a) breakdowns. ☐
    (b) damage. ☐
    (c) both (a) and (b). ☐

Scores: 1st try ☐ 2nd try ☐ 3rd try ☐

Remember to record your scores in the appendix on page 179

Checkpoint answers

1. (a) **2.** (b) **3.** (c) **4.** (b) **5.** (c) **6.** (c)

7. (a) **8.** (b) **9.** (b) **10.** (b) **11.** (a) **12.** (b)

13. (b) **14.** (a) **15.** (c) **16.** (a) **17.** (c)

Instructor's/supervisor's comments: ....

....

....

Stage **4**

Gaining Confidence as You Drive

Introduction

Practise in a quiet area with fairly wide roads, rounded corners and not too many parked cars.

To begin with, learn how to apply the mirror–signal–manoeuvre (MSM) routine for turning left and right into side roads. Practise until you feel confident that you can follow the procedures.

When you have mastered these exercises, practise the MSM routine for approaching and emerging from the end of roads. To begin with you should practise at junctions where you will have a clear view into the main road.

When you can cope confidently with the simpler junctions, progress to those with sharper corners and roads with a little more traffic. However, you should still avoid very busy junctions and those on steep uphill gradients.

Don't attempt too much too soon. If things go wrong it will shatter your confidence. Your supervisor must be sure you can cope before taking you on very busy roads, at junctions on hills and those where your view is restricted.

Before going out to practise learn the Highway Code rules listed opposite:

Rule 49	Driving along.
Rules 54–56	Speed limits.
Rule 68	Pedestrians when turning.
Rules 83–87	Markings along the road.
Rule 105	Passing parked vehicles.
Rules 107–108	Pedestrians near junctions.
Rules 107–111	Road junctions.
Rule 117	Turning right.
Rules 121–122	Turning left.

Read pages 27 and 28 of *Your Driving Test*.

Work through this section of the book and complete the checkpoint before going out in the car. Match your answers with those given at the foot of the page. Revise anything you feel doubtful about.

Stage 5

More about the mirror-signal-manoeuvre routine

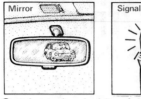

Mirror

Signal

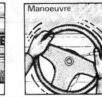

Manoeuvre

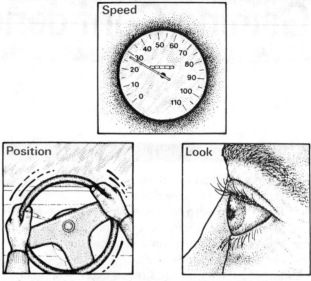

Get into the habit of beginning the mirror–signal–manoeuvre routine early when approaching junctions or other hazards such as obstructions in the road. When you look in the mirror, try to judge the speed and position of vehicles behind. In the early stages, your instructor/supervisor should help you to judge whether your manoeuvre will be safe. Decide whether a signal will help to warn or inform others about your actions. Allow time for them to see and respond to your signals.

A manoeuvre is any action involving a change to your speed or position.

Positioning your car early helps to confirm your signals and intentions. The correct position provides you with the maximum view and safety margins. Others can see you, you can see them and your view of any possible danger is improved.

Try to get your car into position well before you reach a turn or other hazard. This will cause the least inconvenience to the flow of traffic.

Approach junctions and other hazards slowly enough to look for a safe opportunity to proceed. To do this, you will need to slow down before reaching the junction giving you time to select a lower gear ready to accelerate away.

Remember, the brakes are for slowing – the gears for going. Slow down before changing down. If you need to change gear, do it as you finish braking or after you have released the footbrake.

Approaching hazards too fast will result in frequent and unnecessary stops because you won't have time to look properly on the approach.

Start looking early as you approach a junction. Make sure you can see properly before deciding to go forward.

Approaching junctions too fast is often the cause of late, unnecessary stops and unsafe decisions to proceed before the driver can see the way ahead is clear.

Using the MSM routine at junctions

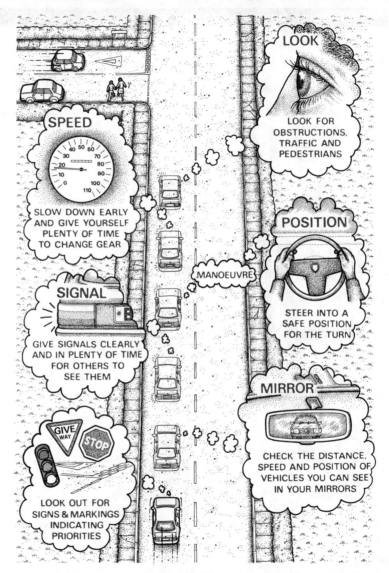

LOOK

LOOK FOR OBSTRUCTIONS, TRAFFIC AND PEDESTRIANS

SPEED

SLOW DOWN EARLY AND GIVE YOURSELF PLENTY OF TIME TO CHANGE GEAR

POSITION

STEER INTO A SAFE POSITION FOR THE TURN

MANOEUVRE

SIGNAL

GIVE SIGNALS CLEARLY AND IN PLENTY OF TIME FOR OTHERS TO SEE THEM

MIRROR

CHECK THE DISTANCE, SPEED AND POSITION OF VEHICLES YOU CAN SEE IN YOUR MIRRORS

GIVE WAY · **STOP**

LOOK OUT FOR SIGNS & MARKINGS INDICATING PRIORITIES

Stage 5

Positioning your car correctly

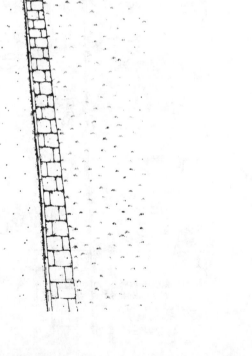

For normal driving, and before turning left, position the car about three feet (a metre) from the kerb. Before turning right, position the car just to the left of the centre of the road.

Be ready to give way to pedestrians

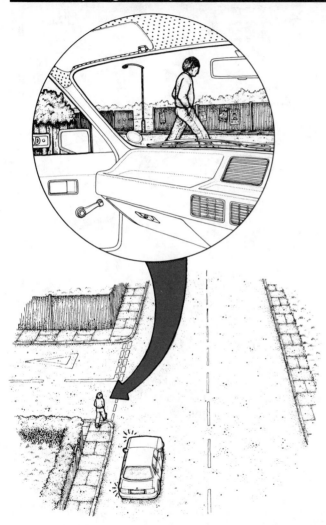

Give way to pedestrians crossing any road you are turning into. Watch out particularly for those with their back to you. They may not have seen or heard you and could walk into the road without looking. In some instances, where they are walking towards the road, it may be appropriate to sound the horn lightly.

Stage 5

How to turn corners

Before taking a hand from the wheel to change gear or use other controls, take a firmer grip with the other hand. Just before reaching a bend or corner, slide the right hand when turning right, or the left hand when turning left, towards the top of the wheel ready to pull it down.

For accurate positioning and steering, it is more important for you to concentrate on where you want to go than on what your hands are doing. Look well ahead into the new road.

Dangers to avoid when turning left

When turning left it is important for you to maintain a position about a metre from the kerb.

If you get too close to the kerb, the rear wheel may cut in and strike it. This could damage the tyre leading to a puncture or result in it becoming illegal to use.

Positioning too close to the kerb may also cause you to swing out into the path of others approaching the end of the road. ▼

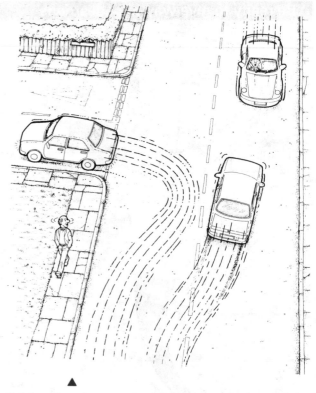

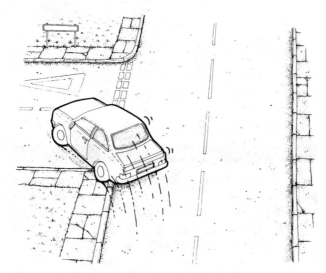

▲

Driving too close to the kerb and swinging out just before you turn could cause following drivers to swerve across the road to pass you.

Positioning your car for turning right

The point of turn

The main danger when turning right is from oncoming traffic. You must normally let approaching vehicles go first. Slow down and hold back until they have passed the junction. If you reach the point of turn first, stop and wait just short of it.

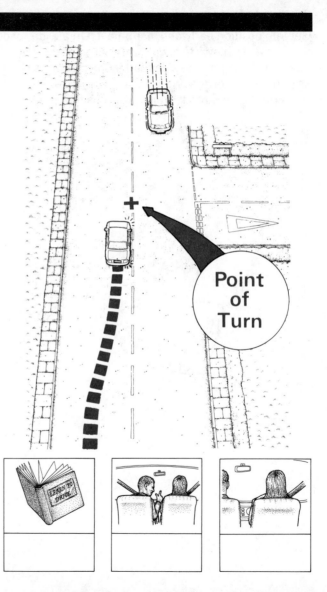

Point
of
Turn

Position before turning right

Get into position early and maintain it. On a wide road this normally allows following vehicles to pass on your nearside. Look into the side road for obstructions such as parked cars or roadworks. Give way to pedestrians crossing the new road. Wait in this position until your way is clear.

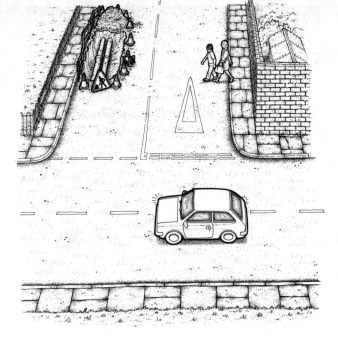

Dangers to avoid when turning right

Remember when turning right the correct position for your car is just to the left of the centre of the road. Maintain this position up to the point of turn and avoid wandering back to the left. ▶

◀ Sometimes you will have to think about turning right from a different position.

Meet oncoming traffic safely. Watch out for vehicles approaching in the middle of the road. Keep well to the left until you can safely move into the correct position for turning.

How to avoid cutting right-hand corners

Move up to the point of turn slowly and make sure you can see into the new road before turning. Avoid cutting the corner and watch out for vehicles approaching the end of the side road.

▼

WHAT IF.....

Pay attention when turning right where your view of oncoming traffic is limited

Cross oncoming traffic safely when turning right. Sometimes your view ahead may be restricted near bends and hill crests. There may be an approaching vehicle just out of sight. Try not to rush across.

Before you commit yourself to the turn, stay in your position just left of the centre until you can see into the new road. Go a little further forwards before turning if necessary.

How to approach the end of a road

Approaching T-junctions

Approach the end of a road slowly, giving yourself plenty of time to look into the main road. There are usually hedges or buildings restricting your view of traffic. If you stop too soon you won't be able to see properly.

Keep a special look-out for cyclists or motorbikes travelling along close to the kerb.

When turning right at the end of a narrow road, position the car well to the left to leave room for traffic turning in.

When you are approaching the end of a road, watch out for others who may be cutting corners. Be prepared to hold back for them.

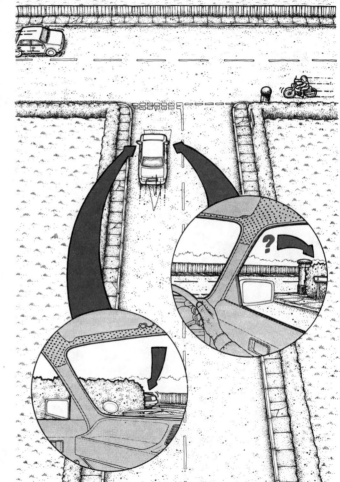

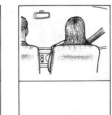

Be ready to give way to pedestrians

When approaching a junction, look out for pedestrians and give way to any who may be crossing the end of the road. Be particularly careful when approaching busy shopping streets.

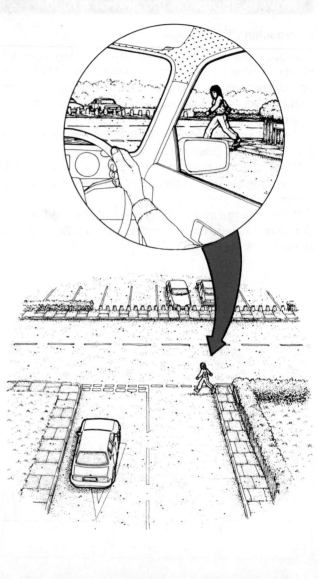

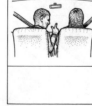

Look both ways before moving into major roads

Vehicles parked near junctions will seriously restrict your view of traffic travelling along the main road.

Creep slowly forwards looking both ways. Look particularly for vehicles hidden behind obstructions. Make sure you can see properly before deciding to proceed.

Watch for vehicles approaching from the left along your side of the road.

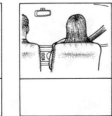

Stage 5

How to approach an uncontrolled crossroad

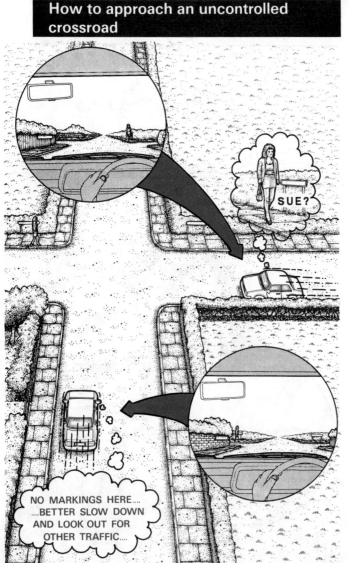

SUE?

NO MARKINGS HERE....
....BETTER SLOW DOWN
AND LOOK OUT FOR
OTHER TRAFFIC....

When driving along quiet side streets you will sometimes see crossroads with no signs or markings.

They are often difficult to spot. Be on the lookout for them. Watch for breaks in the hedges or building lines.

Approach slowly and be prepared to give way to traffic moving along the other road. The other driver may not have seen the danger.

When to give way to oncoming vehicles

When vehicles are parked on your side of the road, check it is safe and move towards the centre without impeding oncoming vehicles. This position will give you a better view ahead and reduce the risk of you getting boxed in. Be ready to slow down early and hold well back to give way to oncoming traffic.

You should normally be prepared to wait in the hold-back position until you can leave three or four feet clearance.

Sometimes, to avoid traffic hold-ups, it may be necessary to proceed through much narrower spaces. To increase your safety margin, feel your way through the gap at a very low creeping speed.

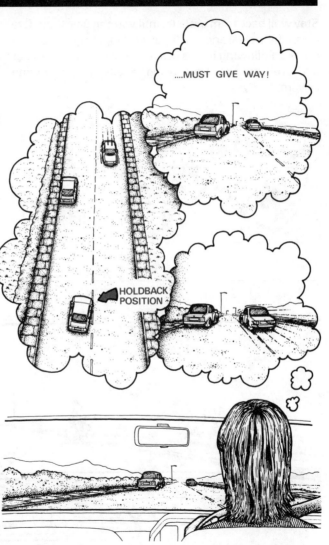

Stage 5

How to follow and pass cyclists safely

Stay well back from cyclists until you can give them five or six feet clearance without endangering oncoming drivers. Following in this position makes passing easier and prevents you from being boxed in by following drivers.

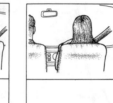

Checkpoint

Using a pencil, tick the box next to the answer you think is correct.

1. The correct position for turning left is:

   (a) as close to the kerb as possible.
   (b) three feet or one metre from the kerb.
   (c) just to the left of the centre line.

2. The correct position for normal driving is:

   (a) as close to the kerb as possible.
   (b) in the centre of your side of the road.
   (c) three feet or one metre from the kerb.

3. The correct hazard routine procedure is:

   (a) mirror–signal–manoeuvre.
   (b) mirror–speed–signal.
   (c) signal–mirror–look.

4. Where pedestrians are crossing the road you are turning into, you should:

   (a) sound your horn loudly.
   (b) hold back and let them cross.
   (c) keep moving until they see you.

5. If there is a 'Stop' sign at the end of the road, you should:

   (a) give way to all traffic in the major road.
   (b) only stop if you can see other traffic.
   (c) stop at the line and give way to other traffic.

6. Approaching a left bend you should position:

   (a) two to three feet or one metre from the kerb.
   (b) towards the centre of the road.
   (c) as close to the kerb as possible.

7. Where there are street lights in a built-up area there is usually a speed limit of:

   (a) 60 mph.
   (b) 40 mph.
   (c) 30 mph.

8. Where you see a national speed limit sign on a single carriageway road the speed limit is:

   (a) 60 mph.
   (b) 50 mph.
   (c) 70 mph.

9. When waiting for a chance to overtake a cyclist should you:

   (a) keep as close to the kerb as possible?
   (b) stay well back from the cyclist but towards the centre of the road?
   (c) get as close as possible so you can pass more quickly?

10. The correct sequence is:

    (a) speed–position–look.
    (b) look–speed–position.
    (c) position–speed–look.

11. The point of turn is:

    (a) the place in the road for waiting to turn right.
    (b) marked with white paint in the centre of the road.
    (c) the point which your wheels must not cross.

12. Approaching parked vehicles you should:

    (a) look for people walking from between them.
    (b) slow down if your view is restricted.
    (c) both (a) and (b).

13. A 'manoeuvre' is any action involving:

    (a) any change in speed.
    (b) any change in direction.
    (c) both (a) and (b).

14. When waiting to emerge into a main road, if you cannot see because of parked cars you should:

    (a) wait for several seconds before proceeding.
    (b) stop at the line and wait until you can see.
    (c) creep forwards until you can see and proceed when safe.

15. The main danger when turning right from a main road is:

    (a) traffic turning left.
    (b) oncoming traffic.
    (c) following traffic.

16. Clearance for parked cars should normally be:

    (a) up to two feet, under a metre.
    (b) three to four feet, a metre.
    (c) six to seven feet, up to two metres.

17. If a car is parked on your side of the road you should normally:

    (a) take right of way over oncoming traffic.
    (b) give priority to oncoming traffic.
    (c) go through quickly to avoid conflict.

18. The position for turning right at the end of a narrow road is:

    (a) just to the left of the centre of the road.
    (b) well in to the left of the road.
    (c) about three feet or a metre from the kerb.

Scores: 1st try ☐ 2nd try ☐ 3rd try ☐

Remember to record your scores in the appendix on page 179

Stage

5

Stage

5

Checkpoint answers

1. (b)	**2.** (c)	**3.** (a)	**4.** (b)	**5.** (c)	**6.** (a)
7. (c)	**8.** (a)	**9.** (b)	**10.** (c)	**11.** (a)	**12.** (c)
13. (c)	**14.** (c)	**15.** (b)	**16.** (b)	**17.** (b)	**18.** (b)

Instructor's/supervisor's comments: ....

....

....

Reversing and Manoeuvring

Introduction

This section consists of a series of structured exercises in manoeuvring the car. You can start practising these when you have reached the end of Stage 4 and are able to control the car at very low speeds with the clutch. The exercises should be introduced progressively with the other subjects you are learning in Stages 4, 5 and 7. You should be able to carry out all the exercises confidently before going on to Stage 8.

During your first few attempts at these exercises, your instructor should make things easier by finding suitable places and also by keeping a lookout for others. This will allow you to concentrate on developing your control and confidence quickly and in safety. If you are learning with friends or relatives, they must also help you initially by looking out for other road users and pedestrians.

As soon as you feel you are able, you must take the responsibility of looking for yourself and making your own decisions as to when it is safe to proceed.

Before going out to practise learn the Highway Code rules 129 to 130; read *Your Driving Test* pages 19, 20 and 21. Work through this section and complete the checkpoint.

Exercise 1 – Revise low speed control

Revise Steps 1 and 2 of Exercise 1 in Stage 4 (page 46) and practise again for a few minutes on a quiet road. Begin practising by slowly driving forwards.

Stage 6

Exercise 2 – How to move out from behind a parked vehicle

A good test to see if you have really mastered the art of controlling the car at low speed, while working briskly on the steering, is to practise moving out from behind a parked vehicle.

Find a vehicle parked on a wide, level road and pull up about 8 to 10 feet (2 to 3 metres) behind it. You will need to control the clutch to move off much more slowly than usual. Take extra observations to the front and rear before you move off and make a final check of the blind spot before you pull out.

Consider whether you will need a signal to warn oncoming drivers as well as any approaching from behind. Use a slipping clutch as practised in Exercise 1 to keep the car creeping very slowly. Turn the wheel boldly until you are clear of the parked vehicle, then turn it back to straighten the car. Remember to look where you want the car to go.

When you have mastered the exercise on a level road practise on up and down slopes, remembering to use the footbrake to control the speed on the downhill ones.

Exercise 3 – How to reverse slowly in a straight line

Practise on a quiet road. Turn round in your seat until you can see the road clearly through the back window. You may remove your seatbelt for reversing if it is restricting you.

You should be able to see the kerb on both sides. Keep a special look-out for pedestrians before you start moving backwards. Look well down the road to the rear as you are reversing. Move slowly back and keep checking to the front and rear for approaching traffic.

To make the car move towards the kerb – steer towards it. To make it move away from the kerb – steer away from it.

If you have taken off your seatbelt remember to put it on again before driving away.

Stage
6

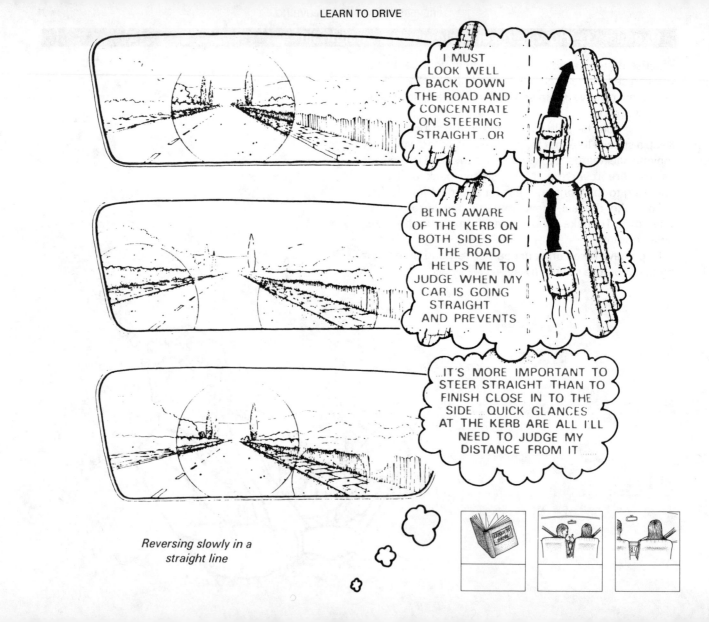

*Reversing slowly in a
straight line*

Exercise 4 - How to drive into a parking space between two vehicles

Look and plan ahead for a suitable parking space. It will need to be at least two and a half times the length of your car. Remember to put the mirror–signal–manoeuvre routine into practice. Slow down almost to a stop just before the space, keeping about a yard (a metre) out from the parked vehicles. Drive on slowly and steer briskly in until your front wheel nears the kerb; then steer right to bring it into line. Centre your car in the space by reversing if necessary.

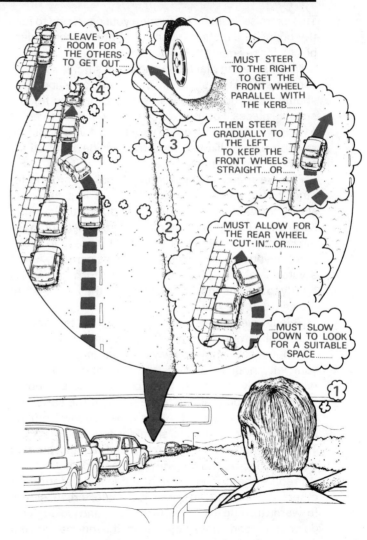

Stage

6

Exercise 5 - How to turn the car round in the road

This exercise is useful for turning your car round to face the opposite direction when there are no convenient places for reversing.

Make sure the place you choose is safe, lawful and convenient. At first, your instructor or supervisor should help you get things right first time by finding suitable places. For this exercise you will need to be on a fairly wide road with only a very slight camber. Before starting, park well away from any roadside obstructions such as trees or lamps.

Prepare the car for moving and look all around for other traffic and pedestrians. When it is safe, creep slowly forwards turning the wheel briskly to the right. Keep checking up and down the road. When you have moved over the centre of the road be ready to brake gently if your car starts rolling down the camber. About a yard (a metre) away from the kerb turn the wheel briskly to the left and stop just short of the kerb. Secure the car with the handbrake.

Select reverse gear and prepare the car for moving. Check all around for other traffic and pedestrians. When it is safe, move slowly backwards, looking over your left shoulder towards the kerb and turning the wheel briskly to the left. Keep checking up and down the road and be ready to brake gently if the car starts rolling down the camber. About a metre away from the kerb look over your right shoulder towards the kerb. Turn the wheel briskly to the right and stop just short of the kerb. Secure the car with the handbrake.

Prepare the car for moving and look all around for others. When you are sure it is safe, creep slowly forwards turning the wheel to the right and looking well down the road, until you are in the normal driving position. Straighten the wheel, follow the mirror-

signal–manoeuvre routine to pull in and park on the left.

If you don't complete the exercise in three movements, don't worry. Simply repeat the second and third movements, remembering to make all the necessary checks for other road users.

Stage 6

Exercise 6 – How to reverse into a road on the left

This exercise is useful for turning your car round to drive in the opposite direction and will also help when you want to reverse into spaces in car parks.

Make sure the place you choose is safe, lawful and convenient. At first, your instructor/supervisor should help you get things right first time by selecting suitable places. To begin with your instructor should find an easy corner for you to practise on and explain what you are going to do while parked on the approach to it.

As you drive past the road check for any obstructions or other problems which may make the exercise unsafe. Using the mirror–signal–manoeuvre routine, stop about two car lengths past the corner and about two feet (just under a metre) away from the kerb.

Turn round in your seat to get a better view to the rear. You may remove your seatbelt if you wish. Check all around for traffic and pedestrians and when it is safe drive slowly backwards until the rear wheels are level with the corner. In a car you can normally judge this by watching for the kerb disappearing from the rear window and then appearing in the corner of the side window.

Before steering round the corner, take a look all around for other road users and pedestrians. Where your manoeuvre will interfere with others, wait and give them priority.

Observations are particularly important just before the front of the car swings out as you steer round the corner. When you start moving back again steer round the corner and keep checking that the side road is clear. Be prepared to pull forwards round the corner again if any vehicles approach from behind to use the junction.

Look through the rear window well down the new road. When your car is almost straight, begin straightening the wheel to bring the car parallel with the kerb. Watch out for people nearby while you drive back two to three car lengths into the new road. Remember, if you want the car to move towards the kerb – steer towards the kerb; if you want it to go out a little – steer away a little. Before stopping, you may glance into the door mirror to check your distance from the kerb.

When you have completed the exercise, secure the car and put your seatbelt on before moving away again.

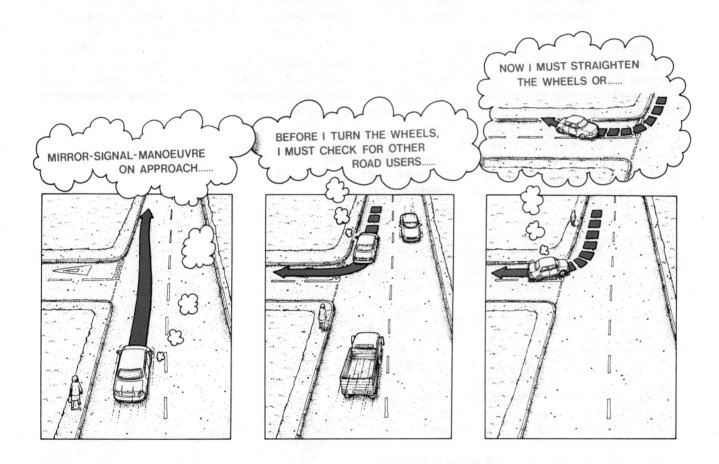

Exercise 7 - How to reverse into a road on the right

This exercise is useful for turning the car round if there is no opening on the left; if you are driving a vehicle without side windows; and for reversing into spaces in car parks.

To begin with, your instructor/supervisor should help you get things right first time by finding easy corners. Park on the left well before the road you will be reversing into so that you can run through the procedure before attempting to practise. Make sure your exercise will be safe, lawful and convenient.

Move off in the normal way and then prepare for taking up a position on the right-hand side of the road. Using the mirror–signal–manoeuvre routine make sure that, if a signal is required, it is timed correctly so that others do not think you are turning right. Wait at the 'point of turn' for any oncoming traffic and then pull over to the right-hand side of the road.

Drive about two car lengths past the corner and stop a little way out from the kerb. It may help to remove your seatbelt and to open your window so that you can look out and see the kerb.

Observations throughout this exercise are extremely important because you are on the wrong side of the road. Look all around for other road users and pedestrians and then, looking through the side/rear window, watch for the rear wheel coming into line with the corner. Using the clutch, pause and have a look all around for others before you start steering round the corner. Remember the front end of the car will swing out.

Creep slowly back, turning the wheel to follow the kerb. When you are round the corner, look through the rear window well down the road. When the car is nearly straight turn the wheel back to bring the car

parallel with the kerb. Keep checking all around for others throughout the exercise, but concentrating on looking over your left shoulder well down the road so that you know if other road users are around.

Reverse for quite a distance in the new road to give you enough time to get back into the correct position to approach the junction to proceed. Remember, you are on the wrong side of the road – check all around before moving away.

  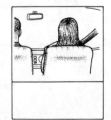

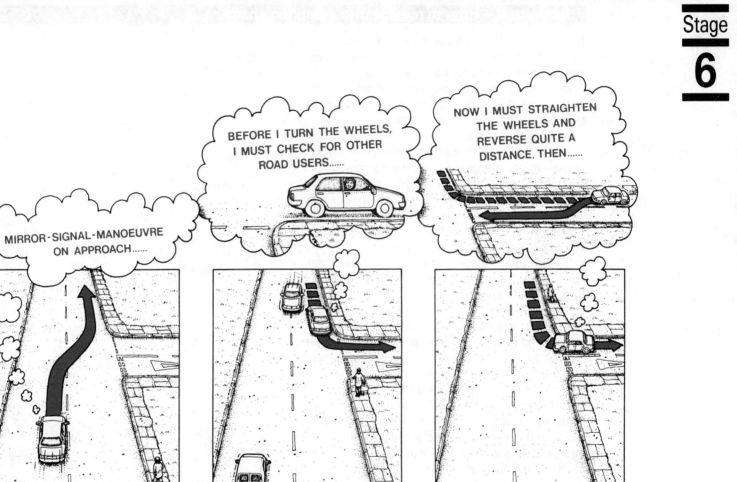

Exercise 8 – How to reverse into a parking space

Before attempting this exercise, you should have had plenty of practice at the other manoeuvres and your car control skills should be well developed.

Make sure the site you select is safe, lawful and convenient. If you are likely to cause a serious disruption to the traffic flow look for somewhere else to park!

Looking well ahead, you will need to find a space at least one and a half times the length of your car. Use the mirror–signal–manoeuvre routine to position for the exercise. There are various ways of telling any following driver that you are stopping to reverse: a left indicator; brake lights; an arm signal for slowing down; and, when you are more proficient, selecting the gear as soon as possible so that the reversing lights come on.

Pull up about three feet (a metre) away from, and level or just forwards of, the front of the vehicle at the far side of the space.

Select reverse gear and check all around for other road users. Reverse slowly until your car is level with the rear of the other vehicle. Pause and check all around again. Turn the wheel briskly to steer your car into the space. When the rear of your car has reached the centre of the space straighten the wheels. Keep moving back with the wheels straight, making sure the front end is clearing the vehicle in front.

When the front end has cleared the vehicle in front, straighten the wheels briskly to bring the front of your car into the space. To complete the exercise centre your car in the space.

Keep checking all around for other road users throughout the exercise – remember they have priority.

MIRROR-SIGNAL-MANOEUVRE ON APPROACH AND STOP LEVEL WITH THE VAN, THEN........

....MUST CHECK FOR OTHER ROAD USERS AND THAT MY FRONT END IS CLEARING THE VAN......

...ONCE I'VE STRAIGHTENED UP, I MUST CENTRE THE CAR IN THE SPACE......

Stage 6

Checkpoint

Using a pencil, tick the box next to the answer you think is correct.

1. Before reversing you should:

   (a) sound the horn.
   (b) make sure the road is clear.
   (c) switch on your hazard warning lights.

2. If you are unable to see when reversing should you:

   (a) sound the horn?
   (b) get someone to help?
   (c) switch on your lights?

3. To turn your car round should you:

   (a) reverse into a side road and drive out?
   (b) drive into a side road and reverse out?
   (c) use driveways to turn in?

4. You should not normally reverse:

   (a) further than 15 yards (14 metres).
   (b) for longer than is necessary.
   (c) where it is safe.

5. When turning your car round in the road you should:

   (a) complete the manoeuvre in three movements.
   (b) keep full control of the vehicle.
   (c) take precedence over other road users.

6. When reversing into a space between parked vehicles you should:

   (a) begin by stopping close to the leading vehicle.
   (b) begin by driving just past the leading vehicle.
   (c) begin by driving well past the leading vehicle.

7. Before driving backwards you should:

   (a) switch on your hazard warning lights.
   (b) ensure no danger will be caused to anyone.
   (c) always remove your seatbelt.

8. When manoeuvring your car you should:

   (a) keep the car moving slowly.
   (b) turn the steering wheel slowly.
   (c) carry out the exercise as fast as possible.

9. Before reversing you should first of all:

   (a) turn round in your seat.
   (b) remove your seatbelt.
   (c) take off the handbrake.

10. When parking between two vehicles you should:

    (a) centre your vehicle in the space.
    (b) leave your car closer to the one in front.
    (c) leave your car closer to the one behind.

11. When reversing you should normally:

    (a) take precedence over other road users.
    (b) give way to other road users.
    (c) ignore other road users.

12. Reversing into a road on the right is useful if:

    (a) the road is very wide.
    (b) you are in a saloon car.
    (c) you are driving a van without side windows.

13. Reversing into a parking space between two other parked vehicles requires at least:

    (a) three times the length of your car.
    (b) two and a half times the length of your car.
    (c) one and a half times the length of your car.

Scores: 1st try ☐ 2nd try ☐ 3rd try ☐

Remember to record your scores in the appendix on page 179

Checkpoint answers

1. (b) **2.** (b) **3.** (a) **4.** (b) **5.** (b) **6.** (b)
7. (b) **8.** (a) **9.** (a) **10.** (a) **11.** (b) **12.** (c)
13. (c)

Instructor's/supervisor's comments: ....
....
....

Using Common Sense and Gaining Experience

Introduction

When you have mastered the car control skills and the basic rules and routine procedures outlined in Stage 5, you should begin to gain experience on busier roads with more traffic.

You may feel a little anxious about this at first, but try to keep calm and take things one step at a time. The only way to build your confidence in these conditions is to practise in them. At first, you should practise in your nearest town or on the outskirts of a city. Gradually work your way nearer to the town centre as your confidence increases.

Try to get plenty of experience on a wide variety of roads and junctions. If you live in a rural area your instructor may advise you to have longer lessons so that you can gain some experience in the busier areas.

Practise driving on roundabouts; in laned traffic; on one-way streets; turning on to and off dual carriageways; and turning right at busy traffic-light controlled crossroads.

Before going out to practise learn the Highway Code rules listed opposite, work through this section and complete the checkpoint. Study *Your Driving Test* pages 22 to 37.

Rules 71–75	Zebra and pelican crossings.
Rules 87–98	Driving in lanes.
Rules 99–106	Overtaking.
Rule 112	Crossing/turning right into a dual carriageway.
Rule 113	Box junctions.
Rules 114–116	Junctions controlled by traffic lights.
Rules 117–119	Turning right with oncoming traffic turning.
Rule 120	Turning right from a dual carriageway.
Rule 121	Turning left.
Rule 122	Turning across bus lanes.
Rules 123–128	Roundabouts and mini roundabouts.
Rules 225–234	The road user and railway level crossings.
Rules 235–239	Tramways.

Stage

7

How to avoid accidents with other vehicles in front and behind

Follow other vehicles at a safe distance. Stay even further back from large or slow-moving ones. This improves your view of the road and of traffic ahead and helps you to anticipate the actions of the driver in front. You get more time to respond.

When other drivers are following you too closely, drop even further back from the vehicle ahead. This gives you more breathing space and extra time to brake gently; it also gives those behind more time to brake.

Learn to put into practice the 'two-second rule'. When you are following a vehicle, look for an object at the side of the road such as a tree. As the vehicle ahead passes this object say to yourself: 'Only a fool breaks the two second rule'. If you are still speaking as you pass the object, you are following too closely. If you pass it after you have finished, you are keeping a safe distance. Revise Highway Code rule number 57.

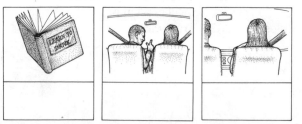

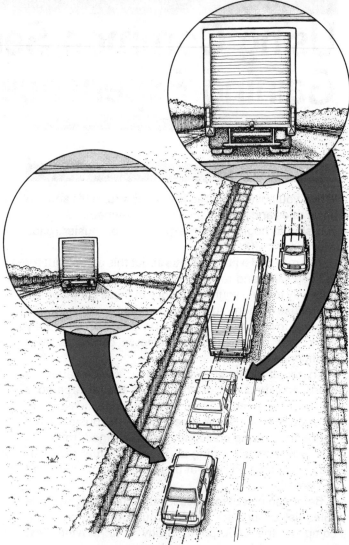

Follow at a safe distance

How to act on signals given by other road users

Watch out for signals given by the drivers of vehicles in front and anticipate their actions. When a signal is flashing, the driver is almost sure to slow down for the manoeuvre. Expect this and carry out your safety routine by checking to see what is happening behind.

If the vehicle ahead is turning right, position your car well to the left and decide whether or not there is room to pass on the nearside. Remember the other driver may have to wait for oncoming traffic. Be prepared to slow down and wait if the space is too small to get through safely.

If the driver in front is signalling left, the vehicle may be either stopping or turning. Move into an overtaking position, but hold well back as drivers waiting in the side road may emerge.

Even when you are sure the driver in front is turning, he may still have to stop and wait if the side road is blocked or if there are any pedestrians crossing. Keep well back.

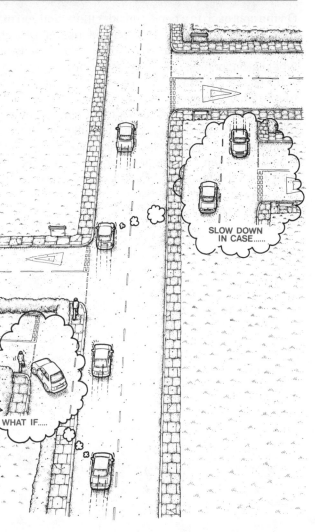

SLOW DOWN IN CASE......

WHAT IF......

Stage 7

Stay alert to what is happening behind

On the approach to a bend, consider the action you may need to take if there is a car parked just out of sight. Check your mirror beforehand so you know in advance what is happening behind. Assess how close other vehicles are, how fast they are travelling and whether they are likely to overtake you.

When the obstruction comes into view, you already have the information to decide instantly whether you need to give a signal. You should also have decided whether it is safe to pull out, or whether you must hold back to let the following driver overtake. Checking the mirror again before pulling out should merely confirm what you already know.

......IS SHE THINKING OF OVERTAKING ME?

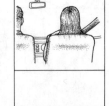

Deciding if you need to signal

Use your mirrors often and, after giving a signal, check to see how others are responding to it.

If you are not sure whether a signal is really necessary, it is usually advisable to give one. Giving a signal, however, will not make an unsafe action safe. Signals do not give you the right to carry out your intentions regardless of others.

Signals are more frequently required for pulling out to pass obstructions when following traffic is approaching quickly, is already in a lane to your right, or when you are driving in fog or poor light conditions.

Indicating too often for passing parked cars can reduce its impact and lull following drivers into ignoring signals given later for turning right. Unless they are too close, following drivers can normally see ahead of you. They can usually judge from your speed and early positioning that you intend to pass parked vehicles.

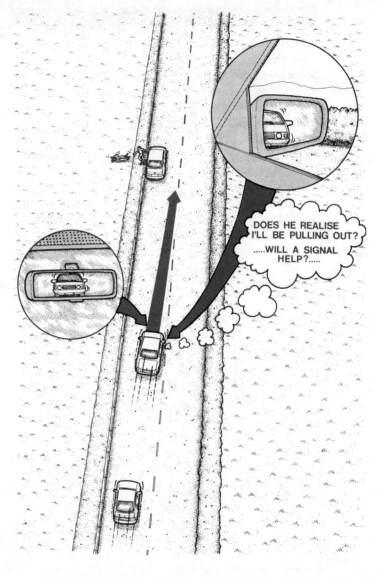

DOES HE REALISE I'LL BE PULLING OUT?

.....WILL A SIGNAL HELP?.....

Deciding when to signal

Signals should normally be given early so that others have time to respond. Some signals, however, need to be delayed; for example, if you want to turn left and have yet to pull out to pass a parked vehicle.

When turning left, wait until you are up to the first road before signalling to take a second. Drivers in the first road may pull out if they think you are turning in. However, try to give as much warning as possible to following drivers.

Signals given at the wrong time may panic others into taking unnecessary evasive action. Before giving any signal you should consider its effect on others. For example, delay a right-turn signal for changing lanes when drivers behind are overtaking you.

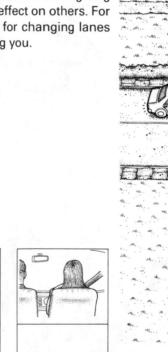

...I CAN SIGNAL NOW

.....MUST DELAY MY SIGNAL, OR......

What to look out for when approaching pedestrian crossings

Look and plan well ahead. Watch out for, and give precedence to, pedestrians on zebra crossings. Look for people standing near or moving towards crossings and try to work out in advance whether they are likely to cross. Check what is happening behind and be ready to slow down. You must be travelling at such a speed that you can pull up safely if they step out.

Watch out for people near crossings

If your view of either side of the crossing is blocked by parked vehicles or other obstructions, slow down as if people were crossing. Be ready to stop until you can see it is safe to continue.

Remember, when you are parking, stop well away from any kind of pedestrian crossing!

Be ready to stop if you cannot see both sides

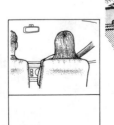

Approaching zebra crossings

Treat a zebra crossing with a refuge in the middle as two separate crossings. If someone steps off the pavement on to the other half you may still proceed. However, you must watch out for anyone nearing the central reserve. They may walk straight through the reserve on to the second half.

You must not overtake on the approach to pedestrian crossings. When driving in laned traffic, where there are vehicles in another lane waiting at a crossing, you may pull level with the leading vehicle but do not proceed in front of it.

How to approach zebra crossings

Look well ahead. Where you see pedestrians waiting to cross, check your mirror and slow down. If you hold back early enough they may have time to go before you reach the crossing. Try to make eye contact with anyone waiting. This helps reassure them that they have been seen.

If you have time, give an arm signal for slowing down. This lets the pedestrians know what you are doing and also warns oncoming drivers that you are stopping. ▼

Do not give any other kind of invitation for people to cross. Other drivers may not be stopping.

Some pedestrians find it more difficult than others to cross the road. For example, you should allow extra time for the old or infirm. Be patient with them. People with prams cannot put a foot on to the crossing to claim priority. They will have to push the pram out. Others with small children also need more time. Young people are often impulsive and may dash out on to the crossing.

If the pedestrians are walking from your right to left, wait until they are on the pavement before moving away. If they are walking from left to right, give precedence to them, but you do not need to wait until they are completely across.

However, do not startle or hurry them by driving too close or too fast. Wait until they are least three quarters of the way over.

Remember before moving away to check to the sides for other pedestrians in your blind spots. ▼

Stage

7

What to do at pelican crossings

Look well ahead and anticipate the lights changing. If green is showing and pedestrians are waiting, they could change very quickly. Check what is happening behind, slow down and be prepared to stop if the lights change.

If the amber light is flashing, give precedence to people who are already on the crossing. When they have crossed you may proceed.

After the lights start flashing, watch out for people making a last-minute dash. Be prepared to let them cross, but do not invite others on to the crossing.

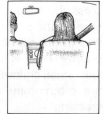

How to approach traffic lights

Plan well ahead. When approaching a red traffic light, check what is happening behind and be prepared to slow down early. This will give the lights time to change and allow you to continue if they do so. If you have to stop, you should normally apply the handbrake and select neutral.

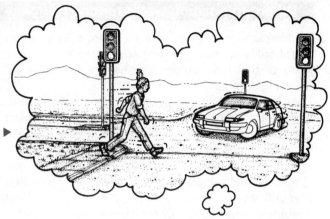

The green light means you may proceed if it is safe. Before proceeding, it is important to check for vehicles proceeding through the junction against the lights. Also look out for any oncoming drivers who might turn right across your path. Watch out for pedestrians crossing the road you are turning into and be prepared to hold back for them.

If your intended exit is blocked, wait at the stop line until you can move through the junction without blocking it yourself.

Remember that all the other colours except green mean stop. Try to anticipate the possibility of a green light changing and be ready to pull up. At some point on the approach, however, you will find yourself too close to stop safely. When you have passed this point you should normally continue.

Working things out as you approach will help speed up your reactions. Check how close following vehicles are and how fast they are travelling. Continually reassess what you will do if the lights change. This will save you time if the amber light comes on by enabling you to make an instant decision either to continue or to pull up.

Stage 7

Where to position when turning or going straight ahead at crossroads

To drive straight ahead or turn left at a busy junction you should normally approach and stay in the left lane. Keep to this lane unless you can see reasons for selecting another.

At junctions with two or more lanes marked with arrows for going straight ahead, plan ahead and choose the most convenient one. To do this look ahead for obstructions and use your knowledge of the area.

To turn right from a busy multi-laned road, you should normally approach in the right-hand lane. One of your first priorities is to get into position early without disrupting other traffic. Check your mirrors for traffic coming up behind and to your sides and time your signal to let others know you want to move to the right. Try to maintain your speed, but be prepared to increase it so you can move safely. Reducing speed may encourage following traffic to overtake and prevent you from carrying out your manoeuvre. If this happens, hold back and wait for a larger space in the traffic. Thinking and planning well ahead should help you avoid becoming boxed in!

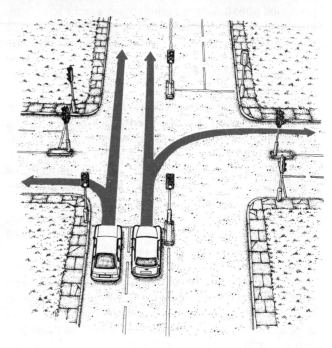

Choosing the most appropriate lane for going straight ahead

Looking and planning ahead will help you select the most appropriate lane for going straight ahead at busy junctions.

If you can see parked vehicles or other obstructions blocking the left lane at the far side of the junction, use the right-hand lane.

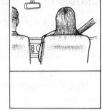

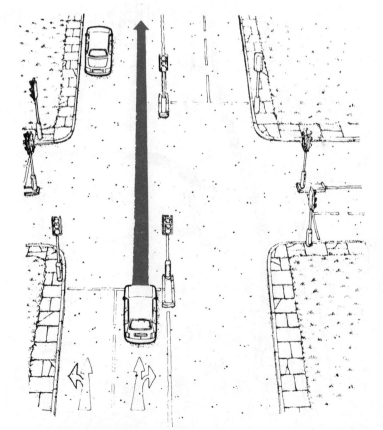

Stage 7

Choosing the most sensible lane

Watch out for right turning vehicles ahead of you. They are sometimes held up for long periods waiting for oncoming traffic. If you position yourself behind them in the right-hand lane, you will also be delayed.

In this situation, it is normally better to choose the left lane, even where there are obstructions at the other side of the junction.

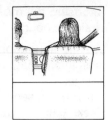

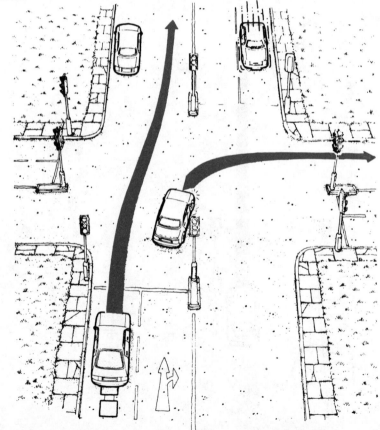

Be prepared to give way to oncoming traffic

When turning right at traffic lights, oncoming vehicles usually have a green light at the same time. Watch out particularly for traffic that is likely to travel straight through the junction or turn left. You must give way to these vehicles as it is their priority.

Wait just short of the point of turn for a suitable break in the traffic. If it is very busy, you may have to wait for the lights to change before you get an opportunity to turn. When this happens you should normally clear the junction as quickly as you can. Make sure, however, that the oncoming traffic is stopping before you proceed.

Stage

7

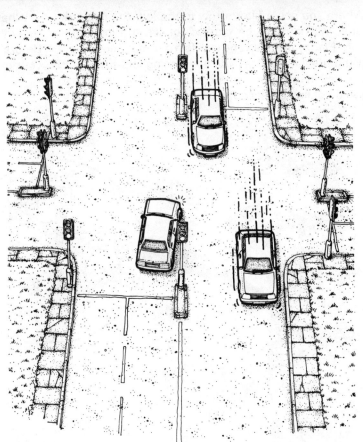

Stage 7

What to do at filter lights

Where you see a filter arrow to the left, the nearside lane will normally be marked for left-turning traffic only. Plan well ahead and look for road markings. Avoid using this lane unless you are turning left. If you find yourself in the wrong lane, continue in that direction to avoid holding other traffic up.

When the filter arrow comes on you may turn left regardless of any other lights which may be showing. Before turning, check for other traffic moving in from your offside.

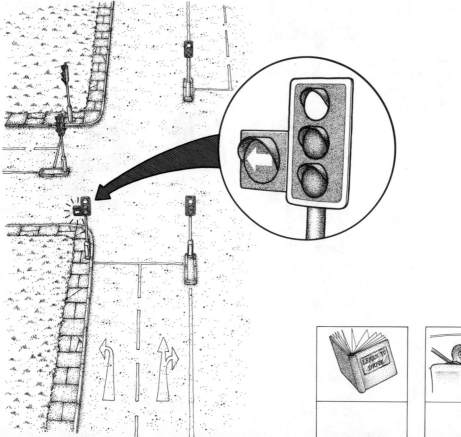

Filtering to the right

Where you see a filter arrow to the right, you may turn right regardless of any other lights showing. Remember, however, that green means go if safe. Check that any oncoming traffic is stopping before you proceed.

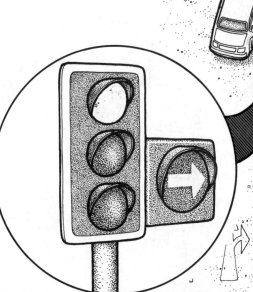

Stage 7

How to deal with box junctions

If your exit road is not clear, wait at the stop line until you can move through the junction without blocking it.

If you are turning right and the exit road is clear, you may enter the box and wait in the centre for any oncoming traffic to pass.

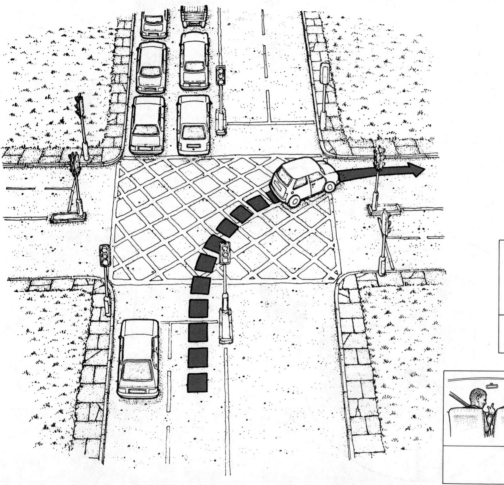

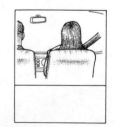

How to choose the most appropriate lane for turning left or right

Look and plan well ahead; and get into position as soon as you can. At some junctions the road markings vary from the normal rules. Where there are two or more lanes marked for the direction you wish to take, choose the most convenient one. To do this you need to know where you should be positioned at the next junction. Look, think ahead and use your knowledge of the area. At first, however, you may have to rely on your instructor for guidance.

Unless you need the right-hand lane at the next junction, it may be more appropriate to select the left lane. However, if you select the right-hand lane for the turn, return to the left as soon as it is safe after completing the turn. Before changing lanes, check there is no one turning at your side. Once you have selected a lane, drive in the middle of it and stay there throughout the turn.

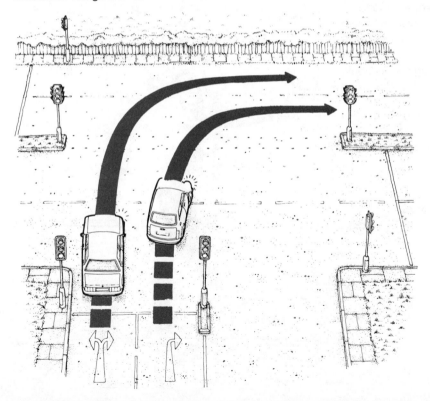

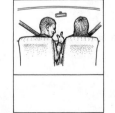

Stage

7

Turning right at traffic lights

There are two methods of turning right at traffic lights where there is oncoming traffic also turning right. The method you select should depend on: the size and layout of the junction; any road markings dictating where to position; how the leading oncoming vehicle is positioned; if you arrive first, you may decide which is the most appropriate method to use.

How to make an offside to offside turn

This method may be appropriate at larger junctions. When the green light appears, move slowly forwards to the point of turn and steer round the rear of the other vehicle. Oncoming vehicles waiting to turn right will severely restrict your view of approaching traffic. Look, and be prepared to wait, for any vehicles travelling through the junction in the far lane.

If you are second in line do not block the road by following the leading vehicle into the centre of the junction. Wait well back until it is safe to proceed. The size of the junction will dictate how many vehicles can wait in the centre.

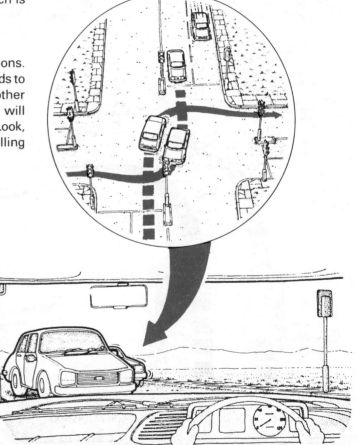

How to make a nearside to nearside turn

This method is sometimes appropriate at smaller junctions. It enables more vehicles to turn in less time and gives an improved view into the new road. When the green light comes on, move slowly forwards, checking the position of the oncoming vehicles. Steer gradually to the right, looking for traffic travelling through the junction. Look, and be prepared to wait, for oncoming traffic in either lane, which may be restricted from your view by other vehicles waiting to turn.

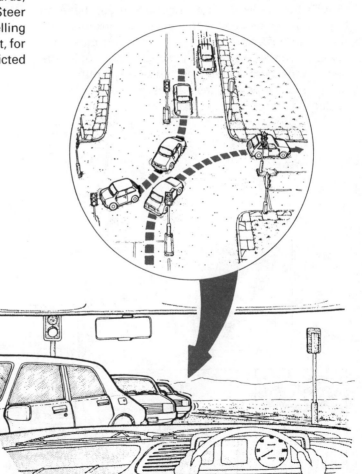

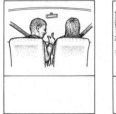

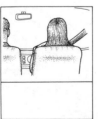

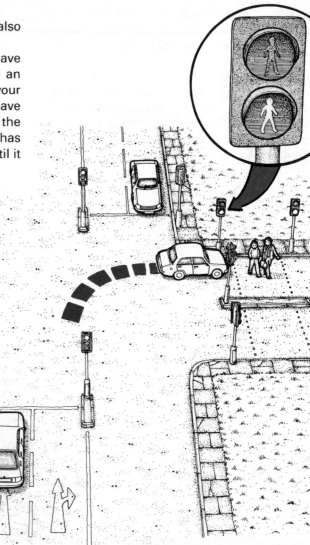

Watch out for traffic-light controlled crossings at junctions

At some larger junctions the traffic lights may also incorporate pedestrian crossings.

When turning right at a busy junction, you may have to wait for the lights to change before you have an opportunity to proceed. If this happens, look into your new road before turning. The green man may have come on and people will start to cross. Look out for the pedestrians and when the oncoming traffic has stopped, pull forwards and wait at the crossing until it is clear.

How to cope with driving in lanes

When driving along dual carriageways and other multi-laned roads drive in the middle of your lane. You should normally keep to the left lane unless turning right or overtaking. However, look and plan well ahead to make sure you don't get boxed in behind any parked vehicles. If you see others wanting to move out into the lane ahead of you, hold back and let them. Avoid straddling the lanes when approaching junctions and passing stationary cars or other obstructions. ▶

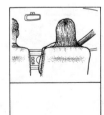

Hold back to let others move out

On one-way streets take the most convenient lane for driving straight ahead and expect traffic passing you on either side. Pedestrians sometimes get confused about which way to look for traffic. Watch out for them stepping into the road, especially if you are in the right-hand lane. ▼

Pedestrians sometimes look the wrong way

109

Stage 7

How to make good use of the mirrors

Simply looking in the mirrors is not sufficient. You must act sensibly on what you see in them. Watch the traffic behind, take note of, and stay alert to, the presence of vehicles moving into the blind spots at your sides.

Let others overtake if they wish and leave room for them to return safely to the lane ahead of you. Remember to use the side mirrors before changing lanes or leaving roundabouts.

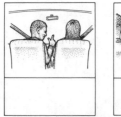

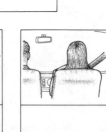

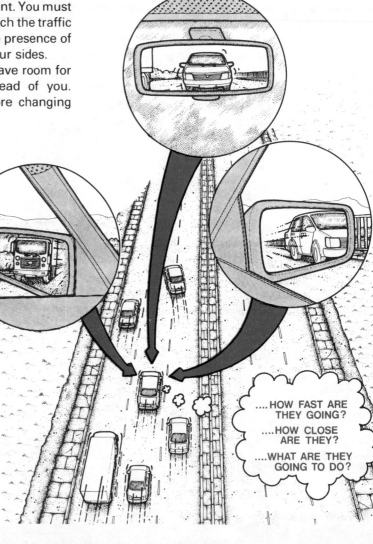

....HOW FAST ARE THEY GOING?

....HOW CLOSE ARE THEY?

....WHAT ARE THEY GOING TO DO?

Driving along dual carriageways

When driving along dual carriageways you must use the mirrors more frequently and plan well ahead. Look for obstructions blocking your lane, vehicles ahead slowing down and those moving through the central reserve.

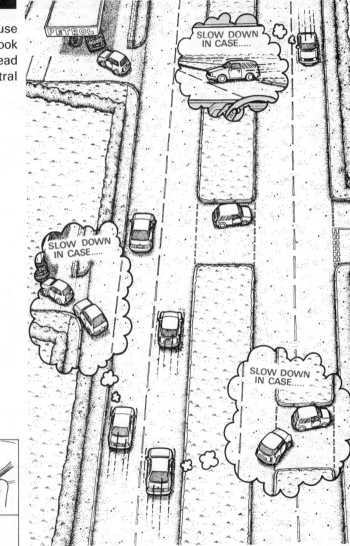

Stage 7

Turning right on to dual carriageways

When turning right on to dual carriageways, decide if there is enough room in the central reserve to offer your car protection from traffic moving along the new road.

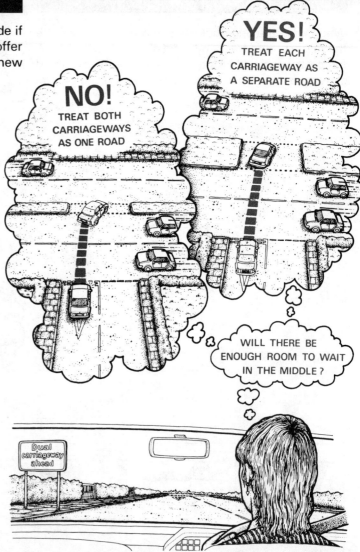

NO! TREAT BOTH CARRIAGEWAYS AS ONE ROAD

YES! TREAT EACH CARRIAGEWAY AS A SEPARATE ROAD

WILL THERE BE ENOUGH ROOM TO WAIT IN THE MIDDLE?

How to approach roundabouts and select an appropriate position

Stage 7

Long before you reach a roundabout, look for the signs to, and make a mental note of, the position of your exit road. Keep checking ahead, making frequent looks to the right as you approach the junction. Try to time your arrival to coincide with a gap in the traffic. Give way to traffic approaching from your right.

When turning left, use the mirror–signal–manoeuvre routine and approach in the left lane. Keep the signal on and stay in the left lane into the exit road.

When following the road ahead, you should normally approach in the left lane and stay in it through the roundabout. As you pass the first exit check the mirrors and give a left signal to indicate you are leaving by the next one.

When turning right, use the mirror–signal–manoeuvre routine to get into the right-hand lane. Keep the signal on and stay in the right-hand lane into and round the roundabout. As you are passing the exit prior to the one to be taken, check for vehicles in the nearside lane and make sure it is safe to cross it. Change the signal to left and leave by the next exit. You should normally leave in the left lane if it is clear.

Stage 7

What to check when leaving a roundabout

Build up and maintain a reasonable speed on the roundabout. Failing to do this, especially when you are in the right-hand lane, may result in other drivers passing on your nearside. Always check for vehicles on your left before leaving a roundabout. If the left-hand lane of the exit road is blocked or there are vehicles in the lane to your nearside, leave in the right-hand lane.

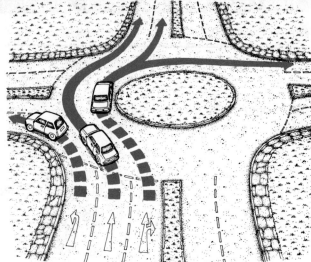

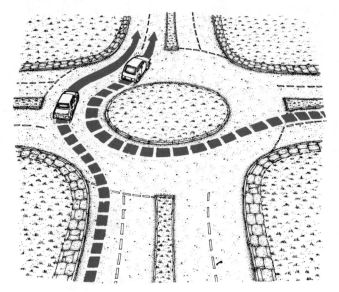

Look well ahead for road markings giving directions that vary from the basic rules. Get into position early and stay in the middle of your lane.

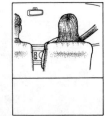

How to plan ahead to the next turn and choose an appropriate lane

You can avoid last-minute changes in position over short distances by working out your course in advance. To do this you need to know where you are going at the next junction and which lane you will need. Look ahead and use your knowledge of the area. At first, however, your instructor should help you with this.

When negotiating a number of junctions within a short distance of each other, choose a lane that puts you in the correct position for the next one. For example, the lane you need to approach the second of these two roundabouts will influence your position at the first. After selecting the correct lane you are able to stay in this lane throughout both turns.

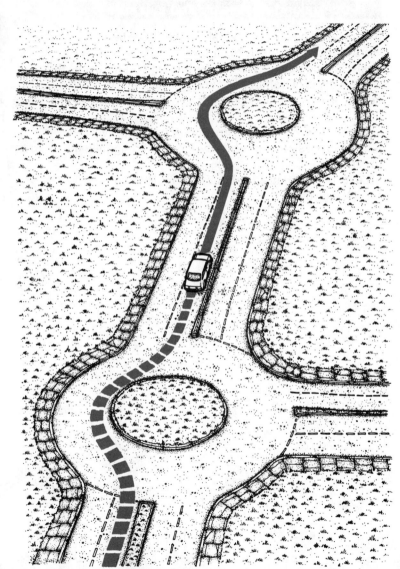

Stage 7

Is overtaking necessary and is it safe?

Before deciding to overtake, ask yourself if the benefit is worth the risk. Is it safe? Is it lawful? Is it necessary? There is little point if you will be turning off shortly, if there is a line of traffic ahead and you will have to slow down, or if the vehicle ahead is driving at the speed limit.

Consider what the other driver may be doing. Will he pull out to pass a parked car or cyclist, or is he signalling to turn?

Last, but not least, is it safe behind? Is someone overtaking you?

THAT DRIVER BEHIND'S THINKING OF OVERTAKING ME!

IT LOOKS SAFE TO GET BY NOW....

Situations in which you must not overtake

Think about the distance you will travel and also about the time you will need to overtake and get back in safely. Consider also the distance that will be covered by any oncoming vehicles.

Do not overtake where your view is restricted by bends or hill crests, or when you are approaching pedestrian crossings and side roads.

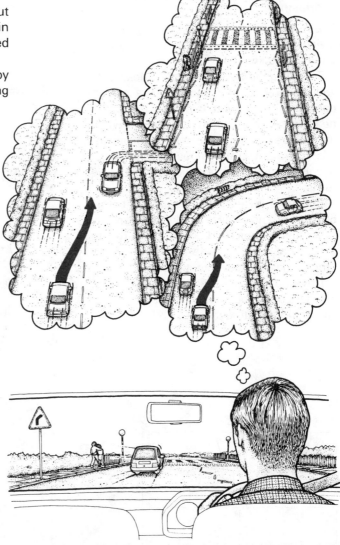

Stage 7

Getting into position to see ahead before overtaking

The mirror–signal–manoeuvre, position–speed–look routine is slightly changed when overtaking.

To get a good view of the road ahead, stay well back and, after checking the mirror, position so that you can look along the nearside. Check the mirror again and, if safe, move over to look along the offside for a long straight stretch of road that is free of oncoming vehicles, obstructions and side turns.

Engage a lower gear, usually 3rd below 50 mph, or 2nd below 20 mph, and be ready to accelerate quickly. Look in the mirror to check that it is still safe and signal to let others know of your intentions.

Drive quickly past and, after overtaking, pull back on to your own side as soon as you can without cutting in.

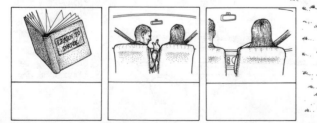

Approaching level crossings

If you see a sign for a level crossing, use the mirror–signal–manoeuvre routine on the approach. A sign should tell you what kind of crossing it is. There may also be distance markers if the crossing is near a bend.

How to deal with gated level crossings

An amber light and ringing sound will be followed by a flashing red light if a train is approaching. The barriers will then come down. You must stop. The red light will continue flashing while the barrier is down. If another train is approaching the lights will continue to flash and the barriers will remain down.

If you break down on a gated level crossing, get yourself and your passengers out of the vehicle, phone the signalman and then, if there is time, push the vehicle across. Stand well clear if the bells and lights come on.

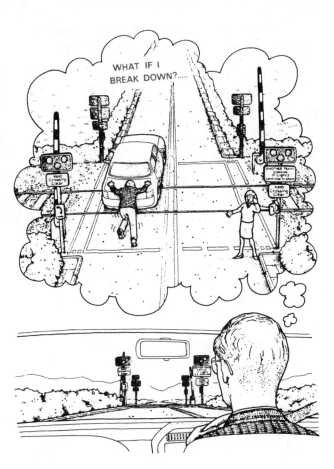

Stage 7

How to deal with an ungated level crossing

Some level crossings do not have gates or barriers. These will have either flashing traffic lights or 'Give Way' signs.

If for any reason you cannot clear the crossing, do not proceed on to it. A train may be approaching.

Checkpoint

Using a pencil, tick the box next to the answer you think is correct.

1. Signals given at the wrong time:

   (a) can be helpful.
   (b) are necessary.
   (c) can be dangerous.

2. On a multi-laned road you should normally:

   (a) drive in the centre lane.
   (b) drive in the left lane.
   (c) drive in the centre of the carriageway.

3. When following the road ahead at a roundabout with three lanes you should:

   (a) normally use the left lane.
   (b) normally use the right lane.
   (c) normally use the centre lane.

4. When leaving a roundabout you should normally:

   (a) take the left lane.
   (b) take the right lane.
   (c) take the centre lane.

5. If you get into the wrong lane at a junction you should:

   (a) proceed in the direction of that lane.
   (b) pull up and wait until you can change lanes.
   (c) signal and move over quickly.

6. When driving in lanes you should:

   (a) keep to the left of the lane.
   (b) keep to the right of the lane.
   (c) position in the centre of the lane.

7. On one-way streets you should expect:

   (a) pedestrians walking into the road looking the other way.
   (b) vehicles overtaking you on either side.
   (c) both (a) and (b).

8. The flashing amber light at a pelican crossing means:

   (a) give way to pedestrians on the crossing.
   (b) pedestrians are allowed to start crossing.
   (c) you may beckon pedestrians on to the crossing.

9. Waiting to turn right at a box junction you should normally:

   (a) wait in the box for oncoming traffic.
   (b) wait at the stop line for oncoming traffic.
   (c) wait in the box if your exit road is blocked.

10. Following the road ahead at traffic lights, if your exit road is blocked should you:

    (a) move into the junction and wait?
    (b) wait at the stop line until your exit is clear?
    (c) move over and wait at the back of the queue?

11. When turning right at traffic lights should you normally:

    (a) give way to oncoming traffic?
    (b) wait at the stop line for a break in the traffic?
    (c) proceed regardless of others?

12. A green filter arrow means:

    (a) you may proceed when the main light shows green.
    (b) you may proceed when safe regardless of other lights.
    (c) it is safe for you to proceed.

13. If you break down on a level crossing you should first:

    (a) clear the car of passengers.
    (b) try to push your car clear.
    (c) telephone the signalman.

14. Arm signals are useful when:

    (a) taking your driving test.
    (b) passing parked vehicles.
    (c) slowing down at zebra crossings.

15. You should give precedence to pedestrians:

    (a) on zebra crossings.
    (b) waiting to cross at pelican crossings.
    (c) at all times.

16. A zebra crossing with a central refuge should:

    (a) be treated as one continuous crossing.
    (b) be treated as two separate crossings.
    (c) be treated the same as one without a refuge.

17. Dual carriageways are more dangerous than motorways because:

    (a) the traffic travels much faster.
    (b) traffic may turn right from them.
    (c) traffic may overtake on either side.

18. Flashing red lights at level crossings mean:

    (a) stop and wait.
    (b) you have five seconds to cross.
    (c) the gates will fall in five seconds.

19. Turning right across dual carriageways you should:

    (a) wait until you can cross both carriageways in one movement.
    (b) wait until clear to the right, proceed and wait in the centre for a gap in the traffic from the left.
    (c) either (a) or (b), depending on the width of the central reserve and the traffic flow.

Stage 7

20. A safe following distance behind another car is:

    (a) one yard or metre for each mph of your speed.
    (b) two seconds back.
    (c) both (a) and (b).

21. If another driver is following you too closely you should:

    (a) stay further back from the car in front of you.
    (b) flash your brake lights to make him drop back.
    (c) drive faster to get further away.

Scores: 1st try ☐ 2nd try ☐ 3rd try ☐

Remember to record your scores in the appendix on page 179

Checkpoint answers

1. (c)	**2.** (b)	**3.** (a)	**4.** (a)	**5.** (a)	**6.** (c)
7. (c)	**8.** (a)	**9.** (a)	**10.** (b)	**11.** (a)	**12.** (b)
13. (a)	**14.** (c)	**15.** (a)	**16.** (b)	**17.** (b)	**18.** (a)
19. (c)	**20.** (c)	**21.** (a)			

Instructor's/supervisor's comments: ....

....

....

Learning How to Anticipate and Avoid Accidents

Introduction

Road accidents claim far too many lives, leave great numbers of people seriously injured and cost millions of pounds every year.

It has been shown that by learning how to anticipate and avoid problems these accidents can be reduced by as much as 50 per cent.

You should, by now, have dealt with most types of hazard and feel competent to carry out your reversing exercises and other manoeuvres.

You should have discovered from experience that other drivers and road users make mistakes. This section teaches you how to deal with them. It explains some of the ways in which you can learn how to avoid accidents by compensating for the mistakes of other people.

Learn the Highway Code rules listed below. Work through this stage and complete the checkpoint before going out to gain more experience.

Rule 43	Use of microphones and car telephones.
Rule 57	Stopping distances.
Rule 58	Fog code.
Rules 63–76	The safety of pedestrians.
Rule 79	Buses.
Rules 80–1	Animals.
Rule 82	Single track roads.
Rules 131–134	Vehicle lights.
Rule 135	Flashing headlights.
Rule 136	Use of the horn.
Rules 137–144	Waiting and parking.
	Speed limit chart.

Read page 38 of *Your Driving Test* – 'Awareness and Anticipation'.

Stage 8

Facing the consequences of accidents

Accidents cost lives.

No matter who is at fault, or whose priority it may have been, a collision can cause injury, misery and a lot of inconvenience. Be prepared to give way to the aggressive.

It will be of no consequence saying: 'It was the other driver's fault,' if you are injured, you injure someone else or your car is damaged.

If ONLY I'd.....

Being responsible about speed

Try to be a responsible and caring driver. Be sensible and safe about where, and how to use speed. When you double your speed, remember that your braking distance increases by four times.

Driving too fast does not mean simply breaking the speed limit. There are many times when the legal limit can be dangerously fast.

Some people may think they are driving at a safe speed for the conditions when really they are going far too quickly. This is usually the result of poorly developed hazard recognition skills and they may be oblivious to the dangers that exist or the risks they are taking.

Stage 8

Stage 8

By now you should have realised that other road users make mistakes. Can you recall any near misses you have had because someone else did something unexpected or foolish? Experienced drivers have learned to anticipate where such things are most likely to happen and adjust their speed to prevent incidents arising. To survive on the roads you must learn to do the same.

As you drive along you must continually look ahead for things that may move into, or across, your path. Think about what could happen if an oncoming car turns right across your path, or a cyclist pulls out of a driveway into the road in front of you.

Look well ahead for obstructions such as parked vehicles. Where your view is restricted there is a risk of other road users you cannot yet see moving into your path. Consider what you will do if a pedestrian runs out. Adjust your speed until you are sure that you will be able to pull up comfortably if it happens.

Be tolerant towards those less skilful than yourself

How well have you learned the Highway Code rules? An understanding of the correct procedures will help you become more confident. Knowledgeable and skilful drivers recognise and react to danger more quickly and decisively than timid ones. Confident drivers are more relaxed, more tolerant and less likely to be frustrated by the mistakes of others. They are less easily provoked by bad manners and less likely to respond aggressively.

Some drivers have the wrong attitude and do not see any need to obey or even learn the rules of the road. They often think it is always their 'right of way'; they are aggressive and quick to lose their tempers. These attitudes are a major cause of road accidents. They can kill.

Be patient. If you behave aggressively you could put other drivers, perhaps less skilful than yourself, under pressure and force them into doing something they are not able to cope with.

Do not let anyone following you too closely force you into going faster than you feel you are capable of. Driving more slowly will reduce any subsequent need for heavy braking and thereby increase the stopping distance for the driver behind.

Keep calm and do not let impatient drivers bully you into moving into a major road against your better judgement.

Avoiding accidents at junctions

Most accidents are the result of a combination of mistakes. Remove any one of these and the accident may be avoided. The accident about to happen in this picture could be avoided by any one of the drivers involved.

The driver turning into the main road looking only to the right is not aware of the vehicle approaching from the left on the wrong side of the road. If this driver looked both ways before emerging the accident would not happen.

Some drivers do not seem to care about the safety of others and park anywhere that is convenient for them. Others may care, but just do not think nor know the rules! Vehicles parked near junctions restrict vision and force others on to the wrong side of the road. If the driver of the parked car had left it in a safer place the accident could be avoided.

The driver moving out to pass the parked car is travelling too fast and has failed to consider the possibility of a vehicle emerging from the side road. If this potential danger is recognised, slowing down and holding back would help avoid the accident.

Concentrate all the time you are driving

Concentrate on your driving. Radios are useful for road and weather reports and for light programmes but serious listening can be a distraction.

Traffic situations can change very quickly and conversation will lower your concentration levels and slow down your reactions. While driving, do not look at your passengers when you talk to them. Stay alert to what is happening on the road all around you at all times.

Keep your hands on the wheel. Fumbling about for matches and lighters, a dropped cigarette or hot ash falling from a pipe, could all result in your losing control of the car. Smoking could kill you a lot sooner than you may think if you do it while driving.

Tuning in to a radio station, changing a tape cassette or using a telephone may mean looking away from the road when you have only one hand on the wheel. Try to avoid these activities while driving, especially at speed, in traffic, and on corners.

If you must answer or make a telephone call, do so when you are stationary.

Stage

8

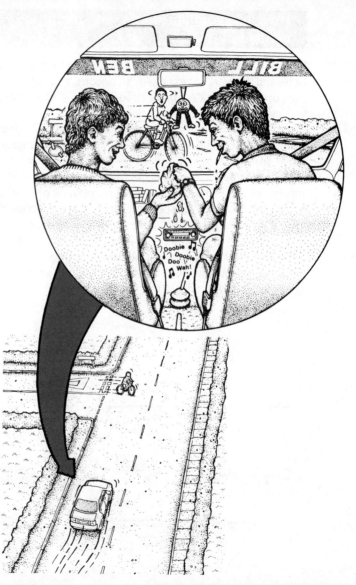

Stage 8

How to avoid accidents with oncoming vehicles

When driving concentrate all the time and look for any potential danger. For example, an oncoming driver may pull on to your side of the road to pass a stationary vehicle.

Work out in advance how this will affect you. Remember that situations sometimes change quickly. Think through how you might be affected by this.

Decide what you can do to reduce the risk. Even though you may technically have priority, be prepared to hold back and compensate for the mistakes, or deficiencies, of others. Will you need to hold back if the oncoming driver moves on to your side of the road?

Use the mirror–signal–manoeuvre routine, find out what is happening behind and judge your approach speed and distance from the hazard.

.....I'M GLAD I SLOWED DOWN TO LET HIM THROUGH!

How to avoid accidents with vehicles turning right

Watch out for oncoming drivers signalling to turn right. If they are nearing their point of turn as you approach, make sure they are holding back for you. Try to make eye contact.

If they are looking the other way expect them to turn across your path. Even though it may be your priority, be prepared to hold back.

When driving in the left-hand lane to go straight ahead at traffic lights watch out for oncoming drivers turning right. They may be unable to see you because of the traffic waiting in the lane to your right.

Stage 8

How to avoid accidents with vehicles emerging from side roads

When approaching side roads, in particular minor crossroads, watch out for drivers approaching the give way lines too quickly to pull up. Be particularly careful, and slow down, where parked vehicles are obscuring your view of junctions, especially where the emerging driver's view may also be restricted.

Where drivers are waiting to emerge from junctions, try to make eye contact with them. This should reduce the risk of them moving out.

Even though you may have priority, be willing to slow down and hold back. Using the mirror–signal–manoeuvre routine, cover your brake and approach the junction at a speed at which you can stop, or at least slow down, if someone pulls out.

How to benefit from using eye contact

When waiting to emerge from a side road into a traffic queue, try to make eye contact with the other drivers. If you can attract their attention with a smile they are likely to let you in.

Stage

8

....IF I CAN CATCH SOMEONE'S EYE.....

.....I'LL LET HIM OUT....

Stage 8

How to change lanes safely in a queue of slow moving traffic

If you find yourself in the wrong lane and are unable to change to another one safely, be prepared to miss your turn until you can move over without difficulty.

When you are in a queue of very slow moving or stationary traffic and you need to change lanes, try making eye contact. Put your signal on and then look at the driver just to your rear. Smile and you will almost certainly be allowed in. Drive slowly and change your direction positively but very gradually. Avoid sudden changes in direction or spurts of speed. Watch out for motorcyclists who may be approaching from behind at high speed between the traffic lanes.

How to avoid accidents with vehicles to your sides

Stay well back from vehicles travelling ahead in the lanes to your sides. Avoid driving in the blind spots of other drivers just ahead of you.

Anticipate the actions of drivers needing to change lanes. Allow them to move into your lane to pass obstructions in theirs.

Be particularly aware that drivers of large vehicles may need to steer an unusual course through some junctions.

Because of the size of their vehicle, they often cut corners at junctions or take unusual courses through roundabouts.

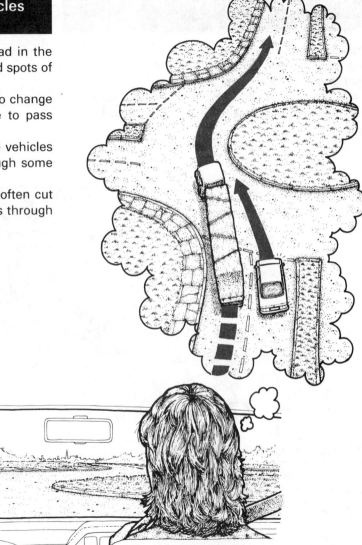

135

Stage

8

Allow room for large vehicles to manoeuvre

Expect large vehicles to swing out before turning left. They may position well over to the left before turning right into a narrow road or entrance.

When you see a large vehicle signalling to turn, hold well back and allow plenty of time and room for it to turn.

How to avoid accidents near buses and stationary vehicles

Expect buses to stop frequently to pick up or set down passengers, often with little or no warning. Stay well back from them and watch out for signals or other signs that they may be pulling in to a bus stop. For example, be prepared for buses to stop if you can see people at a bus stop; or passengers standing on the bus waiting to get off.

If you think the bus is stopping, use the mirror–signal–manoeuvre routine and try to stay in an overtaking position to get a clear view of the road ahead. Hold well back in this central position until you get a safe opportunity to pass.

If you are able to pass, remember your view is ▶ restricted. Be prepared to slow down and watch out for people stepping from behind the bus into the road.

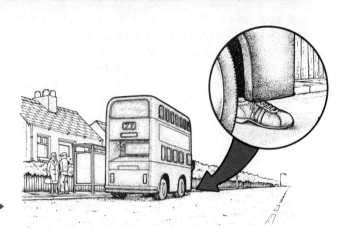

When coming up behind stationary buses, watch out ▶ for the driver signalling to move away. Be prepared to give way where it is safe to do so, particularly when driving in towns.

Stage
8

How to avoid accidents before turning

Use your mirrors frequently as you drive along. Check for any vehicles that may be overtaking you and allow them room to pull back in ahead of you.

Before turning right, check the mirrors for anyone who may be overtaking. Be prepared to slow down or stop and let them pass before you proceed. Remember to time your signals correctly to avoid this problem.

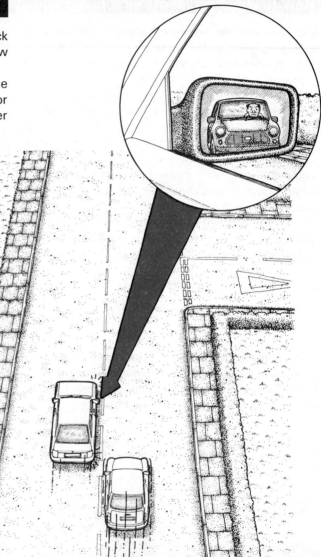

How to avoid accidents near bends and hill crests

Where you cannot see what is there, you do not know what is there!

Where your view of the road is restricted by bends or hill crests, there could be vehicles turning across your path, pedestrians or other obstructions in the road. Be prepared to slow down to ensure you can stop well within the distance you can see to be clear.

There could be an obstruction on the other side of the road and an oncoming vehicle approaching along your side. Be prepared to hold back and give them time to complete their manoeuvre.

Stage 8

What to look out for near parked vehicles

When approaching parked vehicles, try to look through their windows for signs of movement. Leave plenty of clearance and watch for doors opening and people getting out.

Expect other drivers to move out of side roads ahead of you as their view of you may be blocked by obstructions.

Drive more slowly when passing parked cars and watch out for people walking out between them. Try to look underneath the vehicles for feet. Be prepared to slow down as you approach, and hold back for oncoming vehicles.

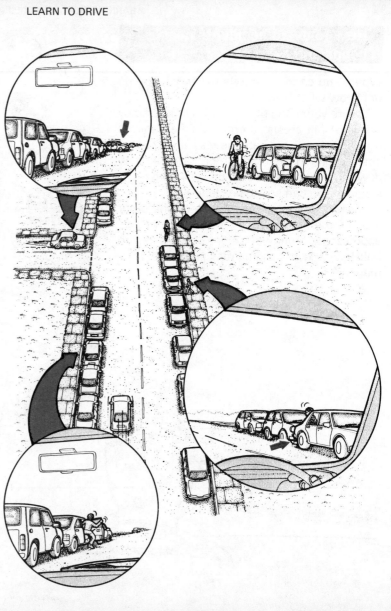

Anticipate the actions of pedestrians

Two out of every three pedestrians killed or seriously injured are either under 15 or over 60. The very young and old often misjudge the speed and distance of approaching vehicles. They may step out unexpectedly into the road.

Be patient with the old, who tend to be slow and hesitant. Show extra care to the disabled and infirm. Look out for blind people with white walking sticks or guide dogs. Remember, too, that some pedestrians are hard of hearing or deaf and may not hear your vehicle approaching.

At all times, watch for pedestrians in or near the road, particularly when driving in shopping streets, when approaching junctions, corners and mobile shops.

Be prepared to slow down and drive with consideration and proper care for their safety. Leave plenty of clearance when passing and approach at a safe speed where they are walking in or near the road. Check your mirror and be ready to stop if necessary. Be prepared to sound your horn to warn them of your presence. Do this as a friendly warning, not as a reprimand.

If you are on a busy shopping street drive more slowly and keep further away from the kerb. Where pedestrians are walking or standing close to the kerb, check your mirrors and be prepared to move further out in the road as you approach them.

Drive slowly near schools, especially at the times when children come and go. Be particularly careful near ice-cream vans and where you see very small children who are not restrained.

Be prepared to move out to avoid pedestrians

How to avoid accidents with pedestrians and children

When you want to turn into a drive or entrance, you must 'give way' to any pedestrians on the footpath.

Be particularly careful before driving out of a blind exit. Be prepared to sound your horn lightly before proceeding.

If you have to reverse out, even more care will be needed. Check that there are no pedestrians around before you move. Drive slowly back and keep looking out for them all of the time.

▼

Children tend to be impulsive and can move very quickly and unexpectedly. They are usually too busy playing to notice what you are doing.

Using the mirror–signal–manoeuvre routine, check on the following traffic and slow down. Be prepared to stop.

Avoiding accidents with people walking in the road

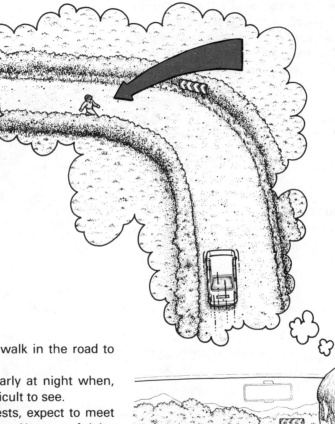

In icy weather pedestrians often walk in the road to avoid slippery pavements.

Watch out for joggers, particularly at night when, even on lit roads, they may be difficult to see.

Approaching bends and hill crests, expect to meet people walking in, or crossing, the road just out of sight. This is common on country roads where there are no footpaths.

Check on the following traffic and be prepared to slow down. Be ready to pull up if necessary or move round them if it is safe.

Stage 8

How to avoid accidents with cyclists

Give cyclists plenty of clearance. The closer you get to them the more they may wobble. If you are unable to pass them with plenty of room, slow down, stay in an overtaking position, and keep well back until you are sure you can get by safely. Allow extra room for them, when riding uphill or steering round grates or potholes.

When you are emerging from junctions look for cyclists riding close to the kerb. Look extra carefully in poor daylight, at night and in bad weather conditions.

Be patient, allowing even more room for children on cycles. The very young sometimes signal for turning one way and then turn the other. Hold back, they are unpredictable.

Some cyclists may ride along on the wrong side of the road or pull out of junctions without looking.

Watch out for children playing around performing unusual manoeuvres such as 'wheelies'.

Anticipate cyclists pulling out to pass stationary vehicles

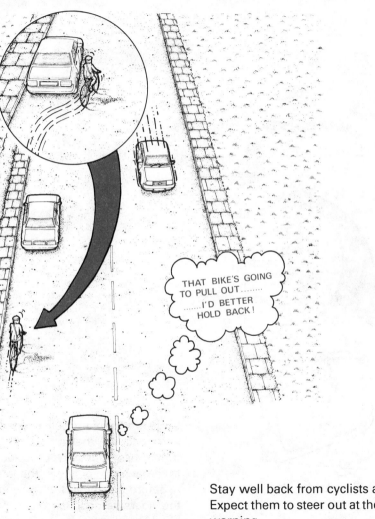

Stay well back from cyclists approaching parked cars. Expect them to steer out at the last minute without any warning.

Using the mirrors to avoid accidents with cyclists and motorcyclists

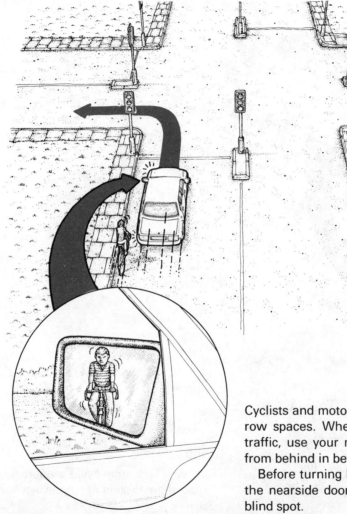

Cyclists and motorcyclists often squeeze through narrow spaces. When driving in lanes of slow-moving traffic, use your mirrors to look for them coming up from behind in between the lanes of vehicles.

Before turning left or moving into the left lane, use the nearside door mirror or look round to check the blind spot.

How to avoid accidents with animals

Expect animals to behave unpredictably. If you see dogs off leads, use the mirror–signal–manoeuvre routine and be prepared to slow down. If one runs out in front of you keep both hands on the wheel, hold the steering on a straight course and brake firmly. When approaching horses, slow down and hold well back until you can leave enough room to pass them safely. Avoid driving by them at speed or with a high revving engine. Do not use the horn as this may frighten them.

How to avoid accidents on country roads

When driving at higher speeds on the open road concentrate hard and plan well ahead. Keep a firmer grip on the wheel and drive a little further out from the edge of the road.

The countryside holds extra dangers. Drive more slowly on narrow roads, through villages and near farm and field entrances. Take extra care at lambing time and when driving through country parks.

Single-track roads are only wide enough for vehicles to move in one direction at a time. Some have special passing places. If you see a vehicle coming the other way, or the driver behind wants to pass you, pull in to one of these. If the passing place is on the other side, wait opposite it.

Be patient behind slow-moving vehicles on narrow roads where it is unsafe to overtake. Expect sharp bends, mud on the road and agricultural vehicles pulling out into your path from fields and farmyards. Drive slowly where your view is restricted. Expect to find pedestrians walking in the road, slower moving traffic, and obstructions.

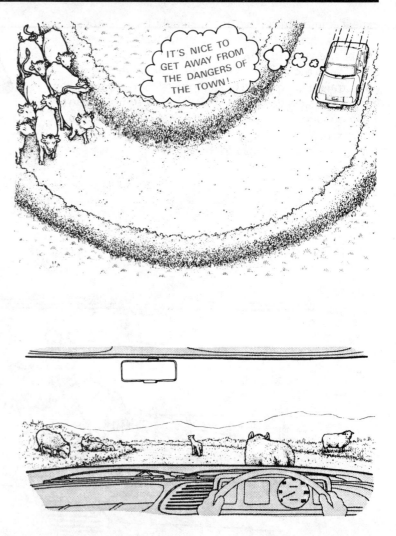

IT'S NICE TO GET AWAY FROM THE DANGERS OF THE TOWN!

Make sure others can see you

Make sure other people can see you at night and in poor daylight conditions by using dipped headlights. Use them in fog, heavy rain and falling snow.

Fog lamps and high intensity lights are extremely helpful in bad visibility. However, if used in the wrong conditions, for example in very light rain, the high intensity rear lights can mask the brake lights and reduce their effectiveness.

IT'S EASIER TO SEE CARS WITH HEADLIGHTS ON IN THESE CONDITIONS...... I WONDER IF THOSE WHO ONLY USE SIDELIGHTS REALISE HOW DIFFICULT THEY ARE TO SEE......

Stage

8

Stage 8

How to avoid accidents when driving in the dark

At night your view is often masked by shadows. Drive more slowly. Watch out for pedestrians, they may be difficult to see when wearing dark clothing. Look out for cyclists who may be riding without lights.

Dip your headlights so as not to dazzle oncoming drivers or the driver of the vehicle ahead of you.

How to avoid accidents when driving in fog

Avoid parking on the road in fog.

If you must drive in fog, use dipped headlights. When waiting to turn right from a major road, keeping your footbrake on may help following drivers to see you.

Watch out for obstructions in the road. Drive at a speed so that you can stop within the distance you can see to be clear. Keep your distance – do not be tempted to drive on the lights of the vehicle ahead.

Use the demisters to keep your windows free of condensation. An open window may also help.

Remember that some drivers may not have their headlights on and it will be difficult to see them until they are very close. Use your ears and listen for other traffic before moving out of junctions. Again an open window may help.

Stage 8

Anticipate the effects of strong side winds

Expect strong side winds when driving in high exposed places or on bridges.

When overtaking high-sided vehicles, hold the steering wheel firmly and be ready to compensate for the wind throwing you off your course as you pass.

When driving in lanes, remember that other road users at your sides will also be affected. Allow extra clearance when passing cyclists.

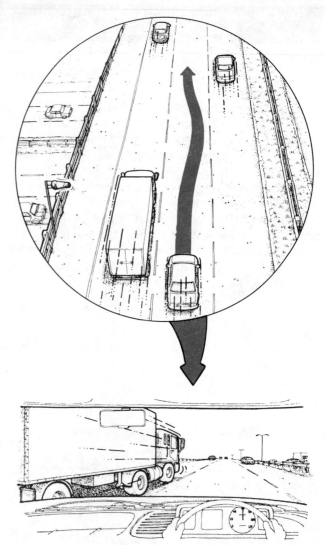

Avoiding problems by reading the road ahead

Read the conditions ahead and slow down well before reaching any bumpy parts of the road particularly where the edges are rough. Keep off soft verges. Look out for mud, loose gravel or chippings.

Following a long spell of dry weather, the combination of oil, rubber, dust and water may make the road surface very slippery after a light shower.

Damp patches on the road under trees are likely to be very greasy, particularly in the autumn. In the winter, these areas will hold frost longer than parts of the road exposed to the sun.

In freezing conditions, avoid accelerating or braking on exposed parts of the road such as bridges. Black ice may have formed.

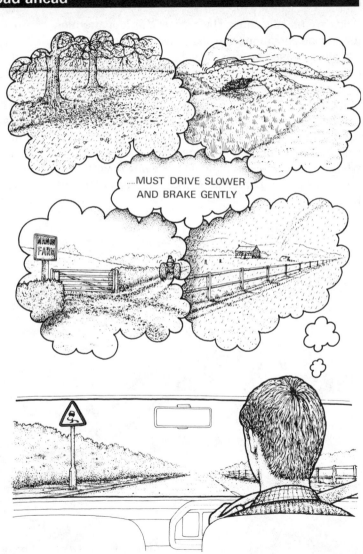

Stage 8

How to avoid skids

Skids are usually caused by a driver's lack of attention to the road conditions and poor driving technique. They are often caused by harsh acceleration, fierce braking, or sudden steering movements, frequently combined with excessive speed.

To avoid skidding, look well ahead, recognise the danger signs and act early enough to avoid sudden or excessive use of the controls. For example, after sighting a group of children near the road, the driver who slows down early, particularly in wet weather, will need less braking pressure if one of them dashes into the road.

Avoid unnecessary journeys in bad weather. If you must drive, remember that your braking distances will be greater. Concentrate all the time. Look well ahead and anticipate the possible actions of others and the road conditions. Be prepared to slow down early. Use the brakes and accelerator progressively.

In snow and ice, slow down early using light braking pressure. Gentle braking is less likely to cause skidding than suddenly changing into a lower gear. Use gradual acceleration and keep in the highest gear possible without distressing the engine. When driving uphill in snow try to maintain a steady momentum by staying well back from the vehicle ahead.

Avoid unnecessary journeys in bad weather

How to deal with fords and floods

When you see a warning sign for a ford, check what is happening behind and slow down. There may be a gauge that will tell you how deep the water is. Select 1st or 2nd gear and, using a slipping clutch, keep the engine revs up. Look for any camber in the road and drive through at the shallowest point.

When you reach the other side, you will need to try your brakes as they may be wet. To dry them out, drive very slowly and press the brake gently with your left foot.

Flooded roads are best avoided. Obey any diversion signs. If you must continue you may need to stop and find out how deep the water is. When you have done this follow the same procedure as for driving through a ford. Drive slowly to avoid any wash that may affect the engine. Test and dry out the brakes afterwards.

Stage

8

How to avoid aquaplaning

Read the road ahead and drive more slowly on wet road surfaces. A cushion of water may build up in front of fast moving tyres. If they are unable to displace the water, they may ride up onto it and lose contact with the road surface in a kind of skiing effect. The steering will become light and the driver may also lose control of the brakes.

To avoid aquaplaning make sure your tyres are kept in good condition, are properly inflated and have the required minimum depth of tread.

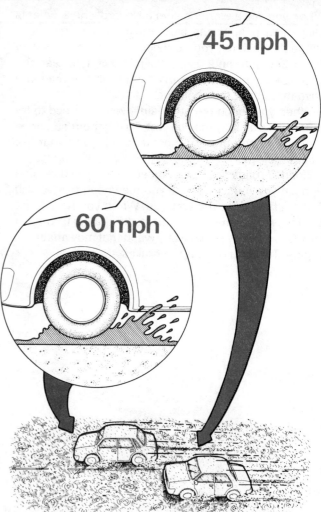

How to correct a skid

The most common types of skid are caused by braking too hard or sudden steering movement at excessive speeds.

Braking too hard may cause the wheels to stop turning. If this happens the car will slide further along the road. An effective remedy is to release the brake and re-apply in a rapid on–off, on–off action.

Attempts to steer round a bend at high speed, particularly in wet conditions, may result in the rear of the car sliding away from the centre of the corner. This rear wheel skid is the most common and is easily recognised because the car goes off course. Your natural reaction should be to steer back on course, but try not to over-react. If the rear of the car swings to the right you should steer right; if it swings to the left, steer left.

Some instructors give training in skid control. Ask yours for information. There are skid pans at various locations throughout the country where specialised instruction and controlled practice in skid correction is available. Ask at your local police station, contact your road safety officer at the county offices, or one of the national motoring organisations for details of skid pans in your area.

Stage 8

Stage 8

Checkpoint

Using a pencil, tick the box next to the answer you think is correct.

1. When driving in fog you should:

   (a) follow the tail-lights of the vehicle ahead.
   (b) use dipped headlights.
   (c) use headlights on full beam.

2. When driving in fog you should:

   (a) allow less time for your journey.
   (b) use your telephone for weather reports.
   (c) allow extra time for your journey.

3. Drivers should give way to pedestrians:

   (a) waiting to cross the road.
   (b) at all times.
   (c) before driving across the footpath.

4. When driving near animals you should:

   (a) be ready to stop.
   (b) sound your horn.
   (c) drive past quickly.

5. Parking on the road at night:

   (a) should be avoided.
   (b) is illegal.
   (c) requires lights to be left on.

6. On a two-lane road if something falls from your car you should normally:

   (a) stop as soon as it is safe.
   (b) remove the article from the road.
   (c) both (a) and (b).

7. The main cause of skidding is:

   (a) the driver.
   (b) the weather conditions.
   (c) the road conditions.

8. Staying well back from a slow-moving vehicle:

   (a) will allow a better view of the road ahead.
   (b) will help you anticipate its actions.
   (c) both (a) and (b).

9. Drivers should normally give way to:

   (a) buses signalling to move out from bus stops on country roads.
   (b) buses signalling to move out from bus stops in towns.
   (c) buses at all times.

10. Approaching a blind bend you should expect:

    (a) pedestrians walking in the road.
    (b) oncoming vehicles to stay on their side of the road.
    (c) other road users to behave correctly.

11. The road surface can be very slippery:

    (a) in the summertime when the weather is fine.
    (b) in damp patches under trees.
    (c) if your tyres are not properly inflated.

12. Wind can affect your vehicle:

    (a) when driving in high exposed places.
    (b) if you keep your windows open at high speed.
    (c) when you have your sunroof open.

13. Driving errors may be caused by:

    (a) the good driver who is concentrating all the time.
    (b) keeping the car in an unroadworthy condition.
    (c) the driver who does not concentrate on the road.

14. If a following driver sounds his horn when you are waiting to emerge from a busy junction you should:

    (a) pull out of the junction as quickly as you can.
    (b) keep calm and wait for a safe gap.
    (c) take as long as you possibly can to teach him a lesson.

15. When driving on a dual carriageway you should:

    (a) only use the interior mirror.
    (b) check the blind spots before stopping.
    (c) use all three mirrors regularly.

Scores: 1st try ☐ 2nd try ☐ 3rd try ☐

Remember to record your scores in the appendix on page 179

Checkpoint answers

1. (b) **2.** (c) **3.** (c) **4.** (a) **5.** (a) **6.** (c)

7. (a) **8.** (c) **9.** (b) **10.** (a) **11.** (b) **12.** (a)

13. (c) **14.** (b) **15.** (c)

Instructor's/supervisor's comments: ....
....
....

Driving at Higher Speeds, Simple Mechanics and Dealing with Emergencies

Introduction

When you have become proficient in all of the previous stages, you should learn to drive with confidence on roads with higher speed limits.

Remember, when you have passed your test you will be entitled to drive on motorways. If you live in an area where there are dual carriageways that carry the national speed limit and that may have access roads similar to those on motorways, you should gain some experience at this type of driving under the safe supervision of your instructor.

Depending on where you live, you may have to travel some distance to reach these types of road, so you may have to have some extended lessons. However, the experience and confidence you gain will be well worth the effort and cost.

It will be your responsibility as a driver to keep your car in a roadworthy condition. You should also know enough about it to be able to carry out simple tasks such as changing a tyre or a bulb, or to be able to recognise when it needs professional attention.

You should know what to do in cases of breakdowns or other emergencies – you may be the first person on the scene!

Before going out to practise learn the Highway Code rules listed below and the sections entitled: 'The Road User and the Law', 'Vehicle Security' and 'First Aid on the Road'.

Rules 149–154	Breakdowns and accidents.
Rules 155–186	Motorway driving.

Work through this section and complete the Checkpoint.

Stage 9

Planning your journey

You should get some experience at driving longer distances and following road signs.

Sometimes it seems that when things start to go wrong, nothing seems to go right. The later you become during your journey, the more others seem to get in the way and all the traffic lights seem to be on red. You begin to lose concentration and become more frustrated. This could lead to anxiety and the likelihood of your taking risks.

You must plan the route and timing of your journey beforehand. Start out early. Allowing yourself plenty of time will give you more opportunity to enjoy the journey and avoid some of the frustration and anxiety that is otherwise likely to build up if there are hold-ups or diversions.

However, even the best laid plans sometimes go wrong. If this should happen, and you find yourself behind schedule, remember that it is far better to arrive late and composed for an appointment than to arrive flustered or, worse still, not to get there at all.

Before setting out on a long, unfamiliar journey, plan the route and jot down the road numbers and towns along the way. Make a note of any motorways and exit numbers.

A route card only takes a few minutes to prepare and it reduces the need for in-car map reading, which will be difficult when you are travelling on your own.

As you drive along, look out for major road numbers and the name of the next big town on green signs (blue for motorway routes). This colour coding helps you to pick out the sign you want more easily. Less important routes and local direction signs have a white background.

Avoid frustration by starting out early

Lane discipline

When you have passed your test you will be permitted to drive on motorways. Practice on dual carriageways will give you some experience at this type of driving.

Some dual carriageways have similar access roads to motorways where you approach on a slip road. Look for a safe gap in the traffic and accelerate until your speed matches that of the vehicles travelling in the nearside lane.

Drive in the left lane. Use the middle- and right-hand lanes for overtaking.

The traffic will generally be travelling faster than you are used to and you will have more things to think about. You will need to plan well ahead. Use your mirrors frequently to check for overtaking traffic and avoid changing lanes unnecessarily.

Be considerate and let others move into the lane ahead of you when they are joining your carriageway from slip roads, where other roads merge and where there are lane closures.

To leave the main carriageway, look well ahead for the signs, get into the left lane in good time. Carry on to the next junction if you miss your exit.

Check your speed before reaching the end of the deceleration lane, you may be travelling faster than you think.

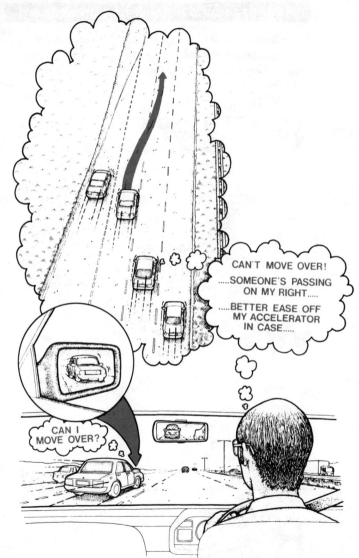

161

Stage 9

How to reduce the risk of a breakdown

Make sure your car is properly maintained according to the manufacturer's recommendations. This will reduce your chances of breaking down or being involved in an accident as a result of mechanical failure.

Before a journey walk around the car and look for any obvious defects such as loose trims, number plates or exhausts hanging down.

Weekly vehicle checks

P is for Petrol. Avoid driving with much less than a quarter tank of fuel. Check this at the start of a journey. Very few service stations are open late at night, and even on trunk roads and motorways there may be long distances between the service areas.

O is for Oil. Check the engine oil and brake fluid. Look for tell-tale oil drips under your car. If the oil pressure or brake warning lights come on while you are driving, stop when safe and get help.

W is for Water. Top up the windscreen washer bottle. Check the radiator coolant level when the engine is cold. Removing the radiator cap when the engine is hot may result in scalding steam and water spraying over you.

E is for Electrics. Check the lights and indicators are working. Carry spare bulbs in the car. These can be changed quickly at the roadside. Make sure the electrolite level in the battery covers the tops of the plates. Top up with distilled water if necessary.

R is for Rubber. Check the pressures when the tyres are cold. Check the tread depth and make sure there are no cuts or bulges in them. Check the spare tyre! Check the fan belt is tight and not frayed. Get the wiper blades replaced if they start smearing the screen.

How to change a wheel

Try to position the car on level, firm ground. Put the ▶
handbrake on, leave the car in gear and switch the
hazard flashers on. If you are on a slope, position a brick
or similar object close to each side of one of the other
wheels to prevent movement. Keep an eye on the other
traffic and take care not to stand in front of your lights
at night.

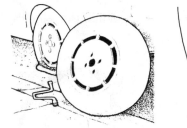

◀ Place the spare wheel, jack and wheelbrace (spanner)
near the tyre to be changed. Loosen the wheelnuts
slightly. If they are too tight you may have to use your
foot and bodyweight on the lever. If you need to do this,
support yourself. If your foot slips you may injure
yourself.

Position the jack under a solid part of the vehicle, or ▶
locate it in the special jacking point shown in your car's
handbook, and then raise the vehicle.

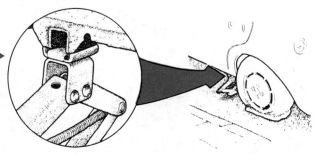

Stage

9

The new tyre will need more ground clearance than the ▶
flat one. Allow for this when jacking up the car. Remove
the loosened nuts and take off the wheel.

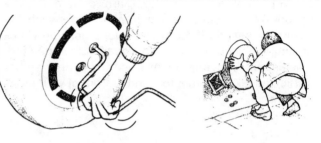

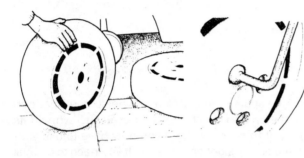

◀ Fit the new wheel and put one of the nuts on
fingertight. Fit the other nuts and tighten them lightly
with the brace.

Lower the jack and tighten the wheelnuts as much as ▶
possible.

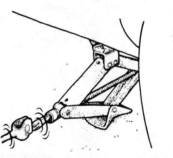

◀ Remove the chocks and remember to put the tools and
wheel in the boot before driving away.
   Check the pressure of the replacement tyre at the
first opportunity.

What to do if you break down

If you should break down, think of others and try to get your vehicle off the road. If you have one, use your car telephone to summon help. Switch on your hazard warning lights and, if you carry a warning triangle or similar device, place this near the kerb about 55 yards (50 metres) behind your car. Do not stand so that you are hiding your lights from others. Display a 'help' pennant. In lonely areas be prepared to lock yourself in the car and speak to others through a slightly open window. If anyone stops to help, ask them to call for assistance for you. If you feel safe enough to go for help, make sure you put all valuables in the boot and lock the car.

For women travelling alone, it is wise to let someone know of your route, destination and estimated time of arrival. In the case of emergencies the police and motoring organisations will give priority to lone women.

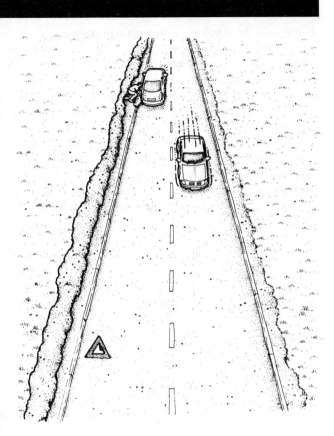

Stage 9

What to do if you break down on a motorway

If your vehicle develops a fault on a motorway, switch on your hazard warning lights and pull on to the hard shoulder as far to the left as possible. If you cannot move your vehicle from the carriageway, warn others of its presence by placing your warning triangle 150 metres to the rear. If you have one, use your car telephone to summon help.

You and all your passengers should leave the vehicle by the nearside door, taking refuge on the bank or nearside land. All doors, except the front nearside should be locked. If the car has central locking, leave it open if there is someone to keep an eye on it.

Stop near an emergency telephone. If you cannot, the arrows on the posts will tell you which way to go for the nearest one. Give full details to the emergency services, making it clear if you are a woman travelling alone.

If you are disabled or if the emergency telephones are out of order stay with your vehicle, display a 'help' pennant, and wait for the special police patrols.

Do not attempt any repairs and do not try to cross the road.

When the problem has been solved, before rejoining the main carriageway, build up your speed on the hard shoulder and look for a safe gap in the traffic.

What to do if you arrive at the scene of an accident

Some knowledge of first aid is useful to any driver because you never know when you may be needed to help. Courses in first aid are run all over the country by the St John Ambulance brigade.

All drivers should carry a first-aid kit in the glove box, where it will be easy to get to. If you arrive at the scene of an accident before anyone else, keep calm. Take charge until someone better qualified arrives. Inform the emergency services immediately, or get someone else to do so.

Talk to those involved in the accident and try to reassure them. Make sure you are familiar with the instructions in the Highway Code under the heading: 'First Aid on the Road'.

Reducing the risk of fire

The risk of fire in modern cars is minimal. However, accident damage can result in broken fuel pipes and leakages on to electrical contacts, causing a spark to start a fire. A 'No smoking' rule should be applied at the scene of an accident and the ignition of any vehicles involved should be switched off.

When you visit a filling station for refuelling, make sure you switch off your ignition and do not smoke.

Many fires in cars are caused by electrical faults. If you suspect any defects get a professional auto-electrical engineer to check over your car.

It is sensible to carry a fire extinguisher. Even if you are not personally involved in an accident, you may come across one where there is a real fire risk.

Stage

9

Vehicle security

Car theft and 'joy riding' are becoming a common nationwide problem. When you leave your car make sure that it and any contents are secure. Lock any valuables out of sight in the boot and remember to wind any aerials down. Park in a safe place and, at night, if it is possible, leave it in a garage or well lit area.

There are lots of safety devices available including: having all the windows etched with the registration number; lockable fuel caps and wheel nuts; steering wheel locks; fuel isolation switches; coded or removable audio equipment; and a variety of alarm systems.

Do not leave the keys in your car, or the engine running, when it is unattended – this is an open invitation to the thief.

If you have to leave a window open for a pet, secure the gap with a grille. This will help deter the thief.

Be alert. If you see anyone acting suspiciously around a parked vehicle, inform the police.

Stage 9

Checkpoint

Using a pencil, tick the box next to the answer you think is correct.

1. If you become tired while driving should you:

   (a) open a window?
   (b) stop at a suitable place and rest?
   (c) either (a) or (b)?

2. Areas of white diagonal stripes painted on the road are to:

   (a) separate opposing streams of traffic.
   (b) protect right-turning traffic.
   (c) both (a) and (b).

3. Red reflective road studs will be found:

   (a) along the right edge of the road.
   (b) along the centre of the road.
   (c) along the left edge of the road.

4. It is more difficult to judge speed and distance:

   (a) in morning mist.
   (b) at dusk.
   (c) both (a) and (b).

5. Overtaking is permitted on the left:

   (a) in one-way streets.
   (b) when turning left at a junction.
   (c) both (a) and (b).

6. When in doubt would you:

   (a) overtake cautiously?
   (b) overtake quickly?
   (c) not overtake?

7. You should not overtake:

   (a) on two-lane highways.
   (b) on dual carriageways.
   (c) near junctions.

8. Overtaking is most dangerous:

   (a) in a built-up area.
   (b) on a country road.
   (c) approaching a bend.

9. When joining a motorway, would you use the slip road to:

   (a) build up your speed?
   (b) look for a safe gap in the traffic?
   (c) both (a) and (b)?

10. When joining a motorway, would you be travelling at:

    (a) 40 mph?
    (b) 50 mph?
    (c) the same speed as traffic in the nearside lane?

11. Learner drivers must not:

    (a) use motorways.
    (b) overtake.
    (c) use dual carriageways.

12. On a motorway, do you normally leave on the:

    (a) left?
    (b) right?
    (c) left or right?

13. On a motorway, something falls from your vehicle, should you:

    (a) stop on the hard shoulder and retrieve it?
    (b) stop on the hard shoulder and phone the police?
    (c) leave at the next exit and inform the police?

14. Flashing red lights above your lane mean:

    (a) do not proceed any further in this lane.
    (b) leave at the next exit.
    (c) move into the next lane.

15. If your vehicle breaks down on a level crossing, would you first:

    (a) push the vehicle clear?
    (b) get your passengers out?
    (c) phone the signalman?

16. If you break down should you first:

    (a) phone for breakdown services?
    (b) think of other traffic?
    (c) get passengers out of the vehicle?

17. Anxiety and frustration can be reduced by:

    (a) starting your journey earlier.
    (b) keeping the car well ventilated.
    (c) taking anti-depressants.

Scores: 1st try ☐ 2nd try ☐ 3rd try ☐

Remember to record your scores in the appendix on page 179

Checkpoint answers

1. (c)	**2.** (c)	**3.** (c)	**4.** (c)	**5.** (c)	**6.** (c)
7. (c)	**8.** (c)	**9.** (c)	**10.** (c)	**11.** (a)	**12.** (a)
13. (b)	**14.** (a)	**15.** (b)	**16.** (b)	**17.** (a)	

Instructor's/supervisor's comments: ....
....
....

The Driving Test

Introduction

While you have been learning to drive you should have been studying: *Your Driving Test*. The syllabus in this book is recommended by the Driving Standards Agency for all learners. Before your instructor conducts your first mock test you should be thoroughly familiar with its contents. If you don't have a copy, your instructor should be able to lend you one or you should be able to buy one from any good bookshop.

The examiner may ask you questions from any part of the Highway Code. Make sure that you are thoroughly familiar with its contents and are able to answer all of the questions at the end of this Stage as well as those you have answered in the other sections of *Learn to Drive*.

Make sure you are prepared for the test. You should feel confident that you are able to drive safely in all conditions without any assistance. If you have listened to your instructor's advice, followed the course instructions, learned the Highway Code thoroughly, and had enough lessons and practice, you should pass quite easily.

Your instructor should help you complete the application form. As soon as you receive your appointment card from the Driving Standards Agency let your instructor know the date, time and test centre. This should ensure that the driving school car is not double booked.

Should you have to postpone or cancel the test appointment you must give the Agency ten clear working days' notice, otherwise you will lose the fee. If you have to cancel on health grounds a medical certificate should be sent.

Read *Your Driving Test*, pages 6–11 and Section 5, page 49

Stage 10

Before the test

As the date of your test gets nearer, your instructor should give you a couple of mock tests. These will show you what to expect and should help to settle your nerves. If you feel over-anxious and make lots of mistakes, it may be a good indication that you need more lessons and practice before taking the real test.

Arriving at the test centre

Your instructor should make sure you arrive at the test centre with plenty of time to park your car and go into the waiting room. If you want to use the toilet, tell your instructor in plenty of time as facilities are not available at all test centres.

Do not worry about feeling a little anxious while you are waiting for your examiner – this is natural.

The test

If you need an interpreter or want your instructor to accompany you on the test, just tell the examiner. He or she should not object. Your examiner will ask you to sign a form, check your driving licence or other means of identity; and enquire if you have any physical disabilities not declared on your application. You will then be asked to read a number plate, after which the examiner will invite you to get into the car. Check it is safe to walk into the road, enter the car and get comfortable.

Examiners understand what it is like to be tested. They are frequently checked themselves by a senior examiner who may sit in on tests. If this happens on your test, just try to concentrate on what is happening on the road, and think about your driving.

During the test

When the examiner has entered the car you will be told to follow the road ahead unless asked to turn, or if road signs direct you to do otherwise. He/she will give you plenty of notice of turns and will not try to trick you into doing something that you should not. For example, if there are two turns on the left and you are asked to take the first available turn, there may be a 'No Entry' sign in the first. Watch out for the signs and act on them. If you are not sure about an instruction ask for it to be repeated.

The first part of the test should be a fairly straight-forward drive. This should give you time to settle down. Your nerves should soon disappear once you get going. Try to have confidence in the examiner and concentrate on your driving or you may worry more about what he is thinking than what you are doing.

Do not try to impress the examiner by being over-careful. If you drive too slowly it may give an impression of lack of confidence. Examiners are not fooled by artificial over-cautiousness. If you are in doubt you should hold back, but try to drive at normal speeds, making safe progress at junctions and in traffic.

Stage 10

Look well ahead and plan your course. Concentrate on what you *must do* to deal with each situation as it arises. Adjust your speed before reaching any traffic hold-ups, junctions and places where your view is restricted. Allow adequate clearance and safety margins and anticipate the actions of other road users moving into or across your path. Use your mirrors frequently and act sensibly on what is happening all around you.

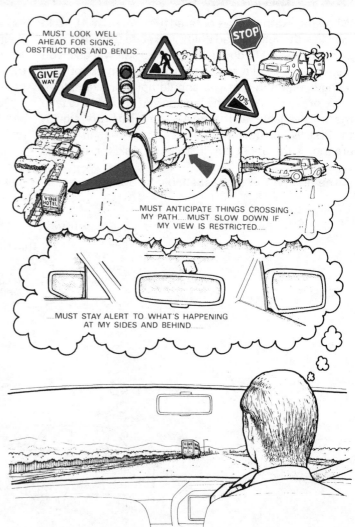

Frequently during your test, the examiner will ask you to pull up at convenient places on the left. This is only to give you further instructions. Remember, however, that it is your responsibility to select safe and legal positions when you stop. If you are asked to pull up just behind a parked vehicle, leave yourself sufficient room for moving off again.

You will be asked to carry out a number of special exercises to demonstrate your ability to handle the car in confined spaces and with regard for other road users.

Special exercises

The first exercise is usually the emergency stop. You will be asked to pull up as if a child has run out in front of you. The examiner will explain the signal for stopping and ask you to drive on again. Keep calm, drive normally and use your mirror frequently. When the signal to stop is given, react promptly and stop quickly and under full control.

You may be asked to reverse into a side road to the left or right. The examiner will ask you to pull up before the corner and give you the instructions for the exercise. If your path into the side road is obstructed in any way, tell the examiner, who will take you to another corner. During the exercise, if your car is going wide or getting too close to the kerb, stop, pull forwards and start again before it gets too late and becomes a serious fault.

You may be asked to turn the car round in the road to face the opposite direction. The examiner will ask you to pull up on the left. Park away from other vehicles and kerbside obstructions such as trees and lamp-posts. If there are obstructions where you stop, be prepared to move away from them before commencing the exercise. The examiner will not mind.

The other exercise is reversing the car into a space of about two car lengths behind another parked vehicle. Remember to use the mirror–signal–manoeuvre routine for getting into position for the exercise. Try to finish with your car parallel with the kerb and reasonably close to it.

Remember that observations throughout all of the manoeuvre exercises are equally as important as your control skills.

Completing the test

When you return to the test centre, the examiner will ask you questions on the Highway Code and other motoring matters. These include identifying pictures of road signs and answering questions on topics such as skidding, parking, vehicle condition and motorways. All you need to do is give common sense replies and show you understand the rules and principles. You may also be asked about situations that arose during the test or to demonstrate arm signals.

Stage 10

After passing your test

If you have followed your instructor's advice we feel sure you will be one of the 750,000 successful candidates out of the 2,000,000 tests conducted each year. Your full licence will permit you to drive in the UK and almost anywhere in Europe.

We hope you will continue to drive to, and strive to improve on, the high standard you have reached.

When you have gained some experience on your own, go back to your instructor for some motorway tuition.

The Advanced Driver's Handbook, written by the authors of this book, and published by Kogan Page, should help you improve your skills.

Why not take an advanced test? Your instructor should be able to advise you on training. Details are also available from:

The Institute of
   Advanced Motorists
IAM House
359 Chiswick High
   Road
London W4 4HS
Tel: 081-994 4403

or RoSPA Advanced
   Drivers' Association
Cannon House
The Priory Queensway
Birmingham B4 6BS
Tel: 021-233 2461

If you fail

The biggest cause of test failure is lack of preparation and practice. Over 1,000,000 people fail every year and we know and sympathise with how they must feel. Did you have enough lessons?

At the end of the test the examiner will explain briefly the main points of failure, highlighting particular areas needing more attention on a 'Statement of Failure'.

The progress and revision section on pages 180–82 is linked to the Driving Standards Agency's marking scheme. Use it to find the appropriate pages in this book, and in *Your Driving Test*, which relate to the faults marked by the examiner. Your instructor will help to interpret the points and advise you on correcting them and improving your overall performance before you take another test.

Checkpoint

Using a pencil, tick the box next to the answer you think is correct.

1. The main items inspected on an MOT vehicle check are:

   (a) engine, gearbox, brakes and tyres.
   (b) brakes, lights, steering and tyres.
   (c) engine, body, brakes and tyres.

2. Engine oil level should normally be checked:

   (a) before every journey.
   (b) at least once a week.
   (c) only at main service intervals.

3. Lights and indicators should be checked:

   (a) every day.
   (b) once a week.
   (c) only at main service intervals.

4. At least once a week, drivers should check:

   (a) radiator coolant level.
   (b) windscreen washer liquid level.
   (c) both (a) and (b).

5. Skidding is caused by the:

   (a) driver.
   (b) weather conditions.
   (c) road surface conditions.

6. A main cause of skidding is:

   (a) excessive speed for the conditions.
   (b) weather conditions.
   (c) road surface conditions.

7. If the rear of your car was skidding to the left, would you:

   (a) steer right?
   (b) steer left?
   (c) hold the wheel still?

8. During an emergency stop your wheels lock and skid, would you:

   (a) release the brake?
   (b) release the brake and then re-apply it?
   (c) apply the handbrake.

9. Tyres must be:

   (a) correctly inflated.
   (b) free of cuts and defects.
   (c) both (a) and (b).

10. Tyres must have a minimum tread of:

    (a) 1.6 mm.
    (b) 1½ mm.
    (c) 2 mm.

11. You may cross the stop line on amber if:

    (a) you are too close to stop safely.
    (b) you can see no one is coming.
    (c) neither (a) nor (b).

12. At traffic lights you may proceed on amber if:

    (a) you have already crossed the stop line.
    (b) you can get across the junction before the other lights change.
    (c) neither (a) nor (b).

13. At a pelican crossing flashing amber means:

    (a) give way to pedestrians waiting to cross.
    (b) give way to pedestrians already crossing.
    (c) neither (a) nor (b).

14. When flashing amber is showing you should:

    (a) proceed if no one is on the crossing.
    (b) give way to pedestrians waiting to cross.
    (c) both (a) and (b).

15. At zebra crossings special consideration should be given to:

    (a) the old and the young.
    (b) people with prams.
    (c) both (a) and (b).

16. A white stick with two red bands means:

    (a) the pedestrian is deaf and dumb.
    (b) the pedestrian is deaf and blind.
    (c) either (a) or (b).

17. Driving past a row of parked vehicles should you look out for:

    (a) pedestrians walking out from between them?
    (b) car doors opening?
    (c) both (a) and (b)?

18. Driving past a row of parked vehicles should you look out for:

    (a) drivers moving off without looking?
    (b) cars emerging from hidden junctions?
    (c) both (a) and (b)?

19. Where pedestrians are crossing the end of a road into which you are turning should you:

    (a) sound your horn?
    (b) give way to them?
    (c) neither (a) nor (b)?

20. Approaching the end of a road should you:

    (a) hold back for pedestrians crossing?
    (b) make the pedestrians wait for you?
    (c) sound your horn?

Stage 10

Stage 10

21. You may sound your horn when stationary if:

    (a) you are testing it. ☐
    (b) you are in danger from a moving vehicle. ☐
    (c) both (a) and (b). ☐

22. You should not sound your horn in a built-up area:

    (a) between 7.30 pm and 11.00 am. ☐
    (b) between 10.00 pm and 10.00 am. ☐
    (c) between 11.30 pm and 7.00 am. ☐

23. If another driver makes a mistake should you:

    (a) flash your lights and sound your horn? ☐
    (b) keep cool and do not react angrily? ☐
    (c) neither (a) nor (b)? ☐

24. Two continuous white lines along the centre of the road mean:

    (a) no overtaking. ☐
    (b) do not cross or straddle the lines. ☐
    (c) no overtaking or crossing the lines. ☐

25. A broken yellow line along the edge of the road means:

    (a) no waiting at any time. ☐
    (b) waiting is limited to the times stated. ☐
    (c) no waiting at weekends. ☐

26. You may stop and wait in a box junction if:

    (a) you are prevented from turning right only by oncoming traffic. ☐
    (b) your exit straight ahead is blocked. ☐
    (c) your exit to the right is blocked. ☐

27. Overtaking is not allowed when:

    (a) driving on two-lane highways. ☐
    (b) driving in a built-up area. ☐
    (c) approaching pedestrian crossings. ☐

28. Countdown markers are found:

    (a) approaching the exits from motorways. ☐
    (b) approaching some roundabouts. ☐
    (c) both (a) and (b). ☐

29. Countdown markers on motorways are:

    (a) blue and white. ☐
    (b) green and white. ☐
    (c) black and white. ☐

30. Countdown markers approaching roundabouts are:

    (a) blue and white. ☐
    (b) green and white. ☐
    (c) black and white. ☐

31. Countdown markers may indicate:

    (a) the distance to a motorway exit. ☐
    (b) the distance to a hazard. ☐
    (c) both (a) and (b). ☐

32. Round signs usually give:

    (a) orders. ☐
    (b) warnings. ☐
    (c) information. ☐

33. Triangular signs usually give:

    (a) orders. ☐
    (b) warnings. ☐
    (c) information. ☐

34. Red circles usually tell you:

    (a) not to do something. ☐
    (b) to do something. ☐
    (c) both (a) and (b). ☐

35. Blue circles usually tell you:

    (a) not to do something. ☐
    (b) to do something. ☐
    (c) neither (a) nor (b). ☐

36. At a mini roundabout, you should:

    (a) give way to traffic from the right. ☐
    (b) give way to all traffic. ☐
    (c) neither (a) nor (b). ☐

37. At a junction with a stop sign you must:

    (a) stop at the line. ☐
    (b) give way at the line. ☐
    (c) creep forwards if the way is clear. ☐

38. The routine sequence for overtaking is:

    (a) mirror, signal, manoeuvre, position, speed, look. ☐
    (b) position, speed, look, mirror, signal, manoeuvre. ☐
    (c) mirror, signal, position, speed, look. ☐

39. Driving in fog should you use:

    (a) headlights on full beam? ☐
    (b) sidelights? ☐
    (c) headlights on dipped beam? ☐

40. If dazzled by someone's lights should you:

    (a) switch off your lights? ☐
    (b) flash your headlights? ☐
    (c) slow down or stop? ☐

41. Following another vehicle at night should you:

    (a) use dipped headlights?
    (b) keep your lights on full beam to be seen?
    (c) use sidelights only?

42. The overall stopping distance at 40 mph is:

    (a) 75 feet/23 metres.
    (b) 120 feet/36 metres.
    (c) 175 feet/53 metres.

43. The overall stopping distance at 70 mph is:

    (a) 175 feet/53 metres.
    (b) 240 feet/73 metres.
    (c) 315 feet/96 metres.

44. The recommended following distance is:

    (a) two seconds.
    (b) one yard for every mile per hour of speed.
    (c) either (a) or (b).

45. If something falls from your car on a motorway should you:

    (a) stop and retrieve it?
    (b) pull up on the hard shoulder and phone the police?
    (c) drive off the motorway at the first exit and contact the police?

46. The biggest cause of driving test failure is:

    (a) taking it before being properly prepared.
    (b) nerves.
    (c) neither (a) nor (b).

47. Driving test examiners pass:

    (a) a specified number of people each week.
    (b) everyone who reaches the required standard.
    (c) a specified number of people who reach the required standard each week.

48. Driving examiners expect test candidates to:

    (a) act like learner drivers.
    (b) drive safely and sensibly.
    (c) drive perfectly.

49. Driving examiners:

    (a) are strict and do not speak.
    (b) try to put you at ease.
    (c) neither (a) nor (b).

50. On a driving test you should:

    (a) be positive and think of the things you should do to deal safely with situations.
    (b) drive extra slowly to show the examiner how careful you can be.
    (c) think about all the things you should not do when driving.

Scores: 1st try ☐ 2nd try ☐ 3rd try ☐

Remember to record your scores in the appendix on page 179

Checkpoint answers

1. (b)	**2.** (b)	**3.** (a)	**4.** (c)	**5.** (a)	**6.** (a)
7. (b)	**8.** (b)	**9.** (c)	**10.** (a)	**11.** (a)	**12.** (a)
13. (b)	**14.** (a)	**15.** (c)	**16.** (b)	**17.** (c)	**18.** (c)
19. (b)	**20.** (a)	**21.** (b)	**22.** (c)	**23.** (b)	**24.** (b)
25. (b)	**26.** (a)	**27.** (c)	**28.** (c)	**29.** (a)	**30.** (b)
31. (c)	**32.** (a)	**33.** (b)	**34.** (a)	**35.** (b)	**36.** (a)
37. (a)	**38.** (b)	**39.** (c)	**40.** (c)	**41.** (a)	**42.** (b)
43. (c)	**44.** (c)	**45.** (b)	**46.** (a)	**47.** (b)	**48.** (b)
49. (b)	**50.** (a)				

Instructor's/supervisor's comments: ....

....

....

Stage

10

Appendix

This section of *Learn to Drive in 10 Easy Stages* is designed to help you build up a picture of your progress. It should help you understand whether you are ready to apply for your driving test or highlight any areas that need further revision and practice.

It is in your own interest not to cheat. You should have answered the questions at the end of each Stage honestly. This will show where there are any weaknesses in your knowledge.

Your instructor or supervisor should also have been frequently checking by asking you questions on the rules and regulations.

Checkpoint scores

As you complete the checkpoint at the end of each Stage, record your scores below. If you cannot answer all of the questions, revise those you are not sure about and try again.

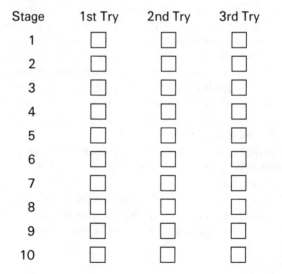

Stage	1st Try	2nd Try	3rd Try
1	☐	☐	☐
2	☐	☐	☐
3	☐	☐	☐
4	☐	☐	☐
5	☐	☐	☐
6	☐	☐	☐
7	☐	☐	☐
8	☐	☐	☐
9	☐	☐	☐
10	☐	☐	☐

'Can do' statements

The driving test is designed so candidates will be able to show they can drive competently and safely, making decisions that will ensure their own safety and that of other road users.

The 'Can do' statements should help you understand and measure your learning achievements. Learning about the rules should help you to make sensible decisions. Your confidence and ability should grow with plenty of practice.

There are three stages in learning to drive. To begin with your instructor will control your actions and tell you exactly what to do. As you improve, your instructor should only need to give you prompts, sometimes just by asking a question. Finally your ability and confidence should have developed so much that all your instructor has to do is check on your performance and give any corrective advice necessary. This is the stage when the responsibility for making decisions has been passed to you and you should be ready for taking your driving test.

You might feel self-assessment is too much bother! However, to get the best value from your training, you will need to be aware of your successes and failures. This will show you where progress is being achieved. You may be surprised to discover that your own markings would not differ too greatly from your instructor's.

As you tick the boxes throughout the text of this book, fill in the dates on the 'Can do' statements table to chart your progress at each lesson or practice session.

Can do statements

Subject	Talk through	Prompted	Unaided
Starting precautions			
Make proper use of:			
accelerator			
clutch			
gears			
footbrake			
handbrake			
steering			
Move off safely			
Emergency stop			
Reverse left			
Reverse right			
Turn in the road			
Reverse park			
Use of mirrors			
Use of signals			
Act on signs/signals			
Making progress			
T Junctions:			
M S M			
speed on approach			
observations			
position/right			
position/left			
Crossroads:			
M S M			
speed on approach			
observations			
position/right			
position/left			
position/ahead			
Roundabouts:			
M S M			
speed on approach			
observations			
position/left			
position/ahead			
position/right			
Meet others			
Safety clearances			
Crossing path of others			
Pedestrian crossings			
Overtaking			
Dual carriageways			
Railway crossings			
Parking			
Anticipating:			
pedestrians			
cyclists			
other drivers			

Tick the appropriate column and make a note of the dates until you improve to the point where you can carry out most of the skills without any help.

Driving test analysis and revision

Use the following list and page references to help organise your revision. The numbers by each item correspond to those on the Statement of Failure form.

1. Read a number plate: *Learn to Drive*, page 18; *Your Driving Test*, page 10.
2. Highway Code rules: *Your Driving Test*, page 11; revise any rules you could not answer.
3. Take proper precautions before starting the engine: *Learn to Drive*, pages 22, 23; *Your Driving Test*, page 12.
4. Make proper use of:
   (i) accelerator: *Learn to Drive*, pages 30, 47; *Your Driving Test*, pages 13, 14.
   (ii) clutch: *Learn to Drive*, pages 31, 32, 33, 46; *Your Driving Test*, pages 13, 14.
   (iii) gears: *Learn to Drive*, pages 28, 29, 38, 48, 49; *Your Driving Test*, pages 13, 14.
   (iv) footbrake: *Learn to Drive*, pages 30, 41, 49, 50; *Your Driving Test*, pages 13, 14.
   (v) handbrake: *Learn to Drive*, page 25; *Your Driving Test*, pages 13, 14.
   (vi) steering: *Learn to Drive*, pages 18, 22, 26, 27, 39, 40, 52; *Your Driving Test*, page 15.
5. Move away safely under control: *Learn to Drive*, pages 37, 46, 47, 74; *Your Driving Test*, page 17.
6. The emergency stop: *Learn to Drive*, pages 51, 52; *Your Driving Test*, page 18.
7. Reversing round a corner to the right or left: *Learn to Drive*, pages 80, 81, 82, 83; *Your Driving Test*, page 19.
8. Turning in the road: *Learn to Drive*, pages 78, 79; *Your Driving Test*, page 21.
9. Reverse parking: *Learn to Drive*, pages 84, 85; *Your Driving Test*, page 20.
10. Using the mirrors: *Learn to Drive*, pages 36, 37, 56, 57, 90, 91, 110, 111, 138; *Your Driving Test*, page 22.
11. Giving signals: *Learn to Drive*, pages 36, 52, 56, 57, 91, 92; *Your Driving Test*, page 23.
12. Acting on signs and signals: *Learn to Drive*, pages 89, 97, 101, 102, 103, 111; *Your Driving Test*, page 24.
13. Exercising care in the use of speed: *Learn to Drive*, pages 42, 89, 125, 130, 131, 132, 139, 140, 143, 147, 148; *Your Driving Test*, page 26.
14. Follow others safely: *Learn to Drive*, page 118; *Your Driving Test*, page 33.
15. Making progress/avoiding undue hesitancy: *Learn to Drive*, pages 109, 112, 171, 172; *Your Driving Test*, pages 25, 26.
16. Acting properly at road junctions:
   (i) regulate speed correctly on the approach: *Learn to Drive*, pages 56, 57, 65, 68; *Your Driving Test*, pages 27, 28, 29.
   (ii) take effective observations before emerging: *Learn to Drive*, pages 65, 66, 67, 68, 112, 113; *Your Driving Test*, pages 27, 28, 29.
   (iii) position correctly before turning right and left: *Learn to Drive*, pages 58, 60, 61, 62, 112–115; *Your Driving Test*, pages 27, 28, 29.
   (iv) avoid cutting right hand corners: *Learn to Drive*, pages 61, 64; *Your Driving Test*, page 32.
17. Overtake, meet, cross the path of other vehicles safely: *Learn to Drive*, pages 61, 63, 64, 68, 69, 94, 100, 101, 103, 106, 107, 109, 110, 117, 118, 130, 135, 136, 145; *Your Driving Test*, pages 29, 30, 31, 32.

18. Position the vehicle correctly: *Learn to Drive*, pages 58, 98, 105, 109, 113, 114, 115, 161; *Your Driving Test*, page 34.

19. Allow adequate clearance to stationary vehicles: *Learn to Drive*, pages 69, 140; *Your Driving Test*, page 31.

20. Take appropriate action at pedestrian crossings: *Learn to Drive*, pages 93, 94, 95, 96, 97, 108; *Your Driving Test*, pages 35, 36.

21. Select a safe position for normal stops: *Learn to Drive*, pages 41, 173; *Your Driving Test*, page 37.

22. Show awareness and anticipation of the actions of pedestrians, cyclists, other drivers: *Learn to Drive*, Stage 8; *Your Driving Test*, page 38.

APPOINTMENTS

Day	Date	Time	£	Sig.

48 Hours' Notice of Cancellation
is Required

Name: ....

Address: ....

....

Driver Number: ....

General Information

Before your first lesson make sure you can read a number plate from 67 feet (20.5m). Read lessons 1 & 2 of Learn to Drive, completing the Checkpoints.

Please bring your driving licence with you on your lessons.

COURSE OUTLINE

Stage 1 Before You Drive   [ ]

Eyesight Checked: ....

Licence Checked: ....

Stage 2 Get to Know The Car
Cockpit Drill   [ ]
Precautions/Starting Engine   [ ]

Stage 3 Starting to Drive
Moving Off   [ ]
Changing up and down the gears   [ ]
Speed and Steering   [ ]
Basic M S M Routines   [ ]
Stopping and Parking   [ ]

Stage 4 Methodical Practice
Ex. 1 Moving Off   [ ]
Ex. 2 Moving Off Downhill   [ ]
Ex. 3 Changing Up the Gears   [ ]
Ex. 4 Changing Down the Gears   [ ]
Ex. 5 Braking/Pausing/Stopping   [ ]
Ex. 6 Emergency Stop   [ ]
Ex. 7 Steering   [ ]

Stage 5 Gaining Confidence
M S M and P S L Routines   [ ]
Position Turning Left/Right Corners   [ ]
Approaching and Emerging/Junctions   [ ]
Approaching Crossroads   [ ]
Giving Way/Holdback Positions   [ ]

Stage 6 Reversing and Manoeuvering
Ex. 1 Low Speed Clutch Control   [ ]
Ex. 2 Moving from Behind Parked Car   [ ]
Ex. 3 Reversing in a Straight Line   [ ]
Ex. 4 Driving into a Parking Space   [ ]
Ex. 5 Turning the Car round   [ ]
Ex. 6 Reversing to the Left   [ ]
Ex. 7 Reversing to the Right   [ ]
Ex. 8 Reverse Parking   [ ]

Stage 7 Commonsense and Experience
Following Others Safely   [ ]
Acting Promptly on Signals   [ ]
Making Effective use of Mirrors   [ ]
Making Proper use of Signals   [ ]
Dealing with Pedestrian Crossings   [ ]
Dealing with Traffic Lights   [ ]
Driving in Lanes   [ ]
Dealing with Roundabouts   [ ]
Overtaking Safely   [ ]
Dealing with Level Crossings   [ ]

Stage 8 Learning to Anticipate
Using Speed Correctly   [ ]
Anticipating the actions of others   [ ]
Being patient and Considerate   [ ]
Avoiding Accidents   [ ]
Concentrate when Driving   [ ]
Using Eye Contact   [ ]
Anticipating Large Vehicles   [ ]
Pedestrians/Cyclists/Animals   [ ]
Poor Visibility/Weather Conditions   [ ]
Vehicle Instability   [ ]

Stage 9 Higher Speeds/Simple Mechanics
Route Planning   [ ]
Driving at Higher Speeds   [ ]
Reducing the risk of Breakdown   [ ]
How to Change a Wheel   [ ]
What to do if You Break Down   [ ]

Stage 10 The Driving Test
Applying for the Test   [ ]
Taking the Test   [ ]
After the Test   [ ]

* * *

Test Applied for on: ....

Test at: .... Centre

Date: .... at .... am/pm

When you go for your driving test, please remember to take your driving licence or, if this is not available, you **must** take some other means of identification.

Sample appointment and progress record card (side one)

Your instructor will record any areas for revision. To locate the correct procedures match the code number with the revision chart in **'Learn to Drive in 10 Easy Stages'**

INSTRUCTOR MARKING CODE

T = Teaching : F = Fair : G = Good
/ = Minor Error : X = Serious Fault

APPOINTMENTS

Day	Date	Time	£	Sig.

Column headings (numbered chart):

1. Meet eyesight requirements
2. Know the Highway Code
3. Precautions starting engine
4. Use of accelerator
4. Use of clutch
4. Use of gears
4. Use of footbrake
4. Use of handbrake
4. Use of steering
5. Move away safely / control
6. Emergency stop
7. Reverse Left / Right
8. Turn in the road
9. Reverse park
10. Use of Mirrors
11. Use of Signals
12. Action on Signs / Markings
13. Care in the use of speed
14. Follow others safely
15. Make progress
15. Avoid hesitancy
16. Juncts / speed on approach
16. Juncts / observations
16. Juncts / position right
16. Juncts / position left
16. Juncts / cutting right corners
17. Overtake other vehicles safely
17. Meet other vehicles safely
17. Cross other vehicles safely
18. Normal driving position
18. Lane discipline
19. Clearance / stationary vehicles
20. Pedestrian crossings
21. Safe position / normal stops
22. Anticipation / other road users

Copyright Autodriva 1993

LEARN TO **DRIVE** IN 10 EASY STAGES

WITH

Sample appointment and progress record card (side two)

Index